next

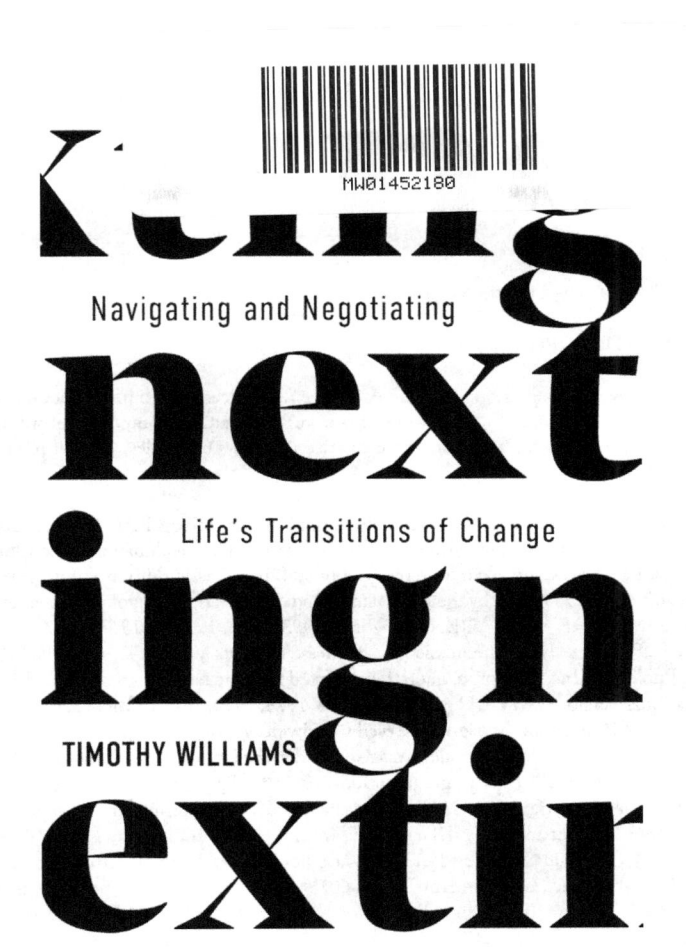

Navigating and Negotiating
Life's Transitions of Change

TIMOTHY WILLIAMS

Copyright © 2024 by Timothy Williams

Published by Dream Releaser Publishing

All rights reserved. No portion of this book may be reproduced, stored in a retrieval system, or transmitted in any form or by any means—electronic, mechanical, photocopy, recording, scanning, or other—except for brief quotations in critical reviews or articles, without prior written permission of the author.

Scripture quotations marked AMP are taken from the Amplified® Bible (AMP), Copyright © 2015 by The Lockman Foundation. Used by permission. www.lockman.org | Scripture quotations marked AMPC are taken from the Amplified Bible, Classic Edition, Copyright © 1954, 1958, 1962, 1964, 1965, 1987 by the Lockman Foundation | Scripture quotations marked MSG are taken from THE MESSAGE, copyright © 1993, 1994, 1995, 1996, 2000, 2001, 2002 by Eugene H. Peterson. Used by permission of NavPress. All rights reserved. Represented by Tyndale House Publishers, Inc. | Scripture quotations marked NIV are taken from the Holy Bible, New International Version®, NIV®. Copyright © 1973, 1978, 1984, 2011 by Biblica, Inc.™ Used by permission of Zondervan. All rights reserved worldwide. www.zondervan.com. The "NIV" and "New International Version" are trademarks registered in the United States Patent and Trademark Office by Biblica, Inc.™ | Scripture quotations marked NKJV are taken from the New King James Version®. Copyright © 1982 by Thomas Nelson. Used by permission. All rights reserved. | Scripture quotations marked NLT are taken from the Holy Bible, New Living Translation, copyright © 1996, 2004, 2015 by Tyndale House Foundation. Used by permission of Tyndale House Publishers, Inc., Carol Stream, Illinois 60188. All rights reserved. | Scripture quotations marked TPT are from The Passion Translation®. Copyright © 2017, 2018 by Passion & Fire Ministries, Inc. Used by permission. All rights reserved. ThePassionTranslation.com.

For foreign and subsidiary rights, contact the author.

Cover design by Sara Young
Cover photo by Andrew van Tilborgh

ISBN: 978-1-957369-95-2   1 2 3 4 5 6 7 8 9 10

Printed in the United States of America

Navigating and Negotiating

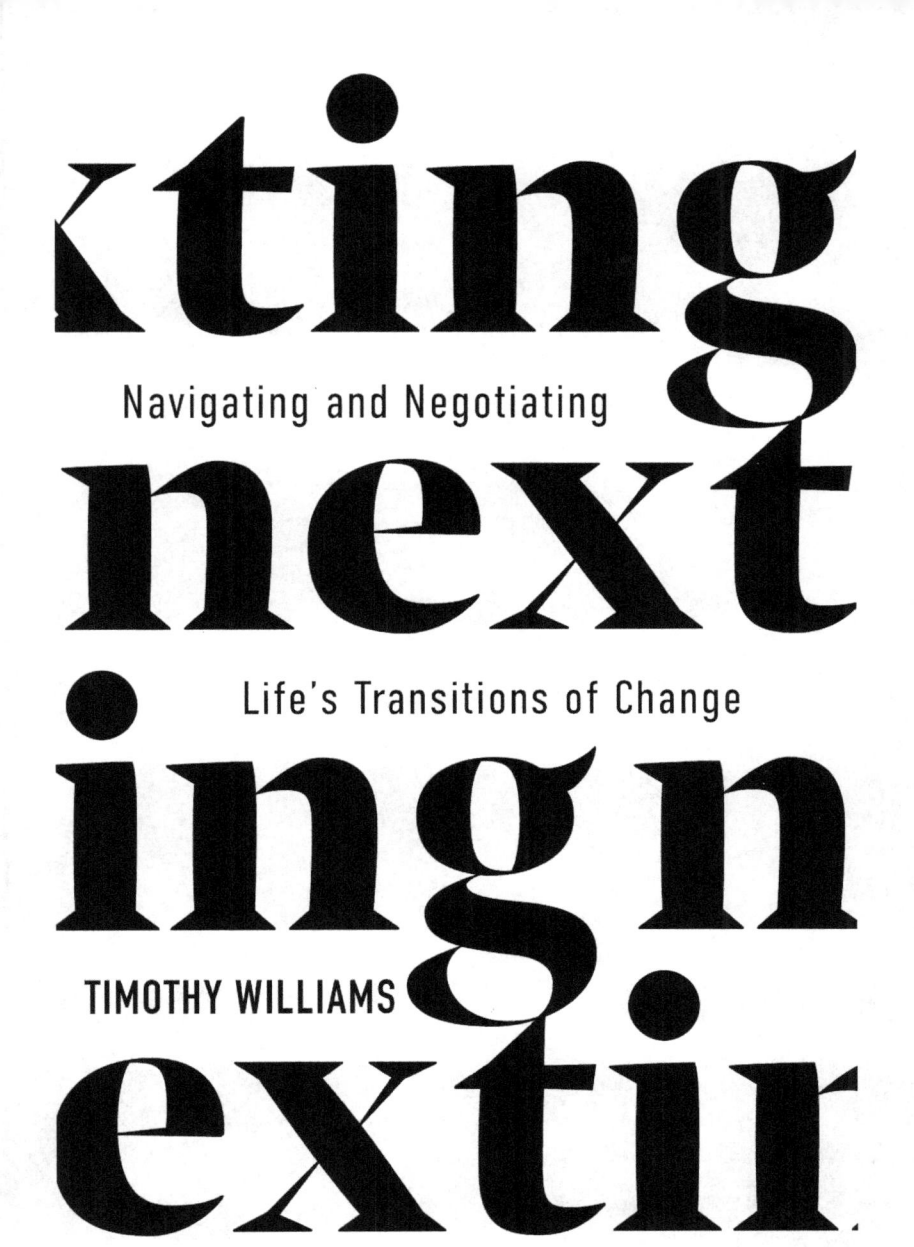

Life's Transitions of Change

TIMOTHY WILLIAMS

DREAM RELEASER PUBLISHING

To my wife "girlfriend", Lisa, who has been "NEXTing" with me for 37 years…

CONTENTS

Introduction 9

PART I. EXPECTING 17
    CHAPTER 1. *NEXTing* as a Concept 19
    CHAPTER 2. The Discovery of *NEXTing* *29*
    CHAPTER 3. *NEXTing* Has a Voice 41
    CHAPTER 4. This Can't Be Happening 49
    CHAPTER 5. What Happens Next Is Very Important ..55

PART II. EMBRACING 63
    CHAPTER 6. The Discipline of *NEXTing* *65*
    CHAPTER 7. Process Then Progress 81
    CHAPTER 8. The In-Between 93
    CHAPTER 9. The Wait (Is a Weight) 115
    CHAPTER 10. Lean Back (A Leaning into) 119
    CHAPTER 11. Don't Allow Next to Hijack Now! 125

PART III. EXPERIENCING 133
    CHAPTER 12. The Dynamics of *NEXTing* *135*
    CHAPTER 13. Transformative Transitions and
                     Assistance 153
    CHAPTER 14. Next is Now 177
    CHAPTER 15. Towards 187

Conclusion 195

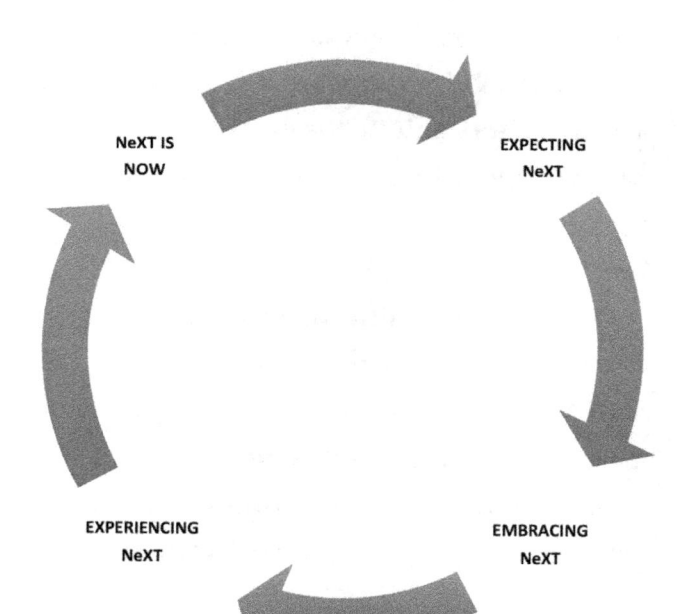

NeXT IS
NOW

EXPECTING
NeXT

EXPERIENCING
NeXT

EMBRACING
NeXT

INTRODUCTION

Welcome to a new beginning in your life! We live life on levels, we arrive in stages, and we experience it in seasons. You are at the beginning of some life-altering shift in your world. Along your journey of life, people, circumstances, and situations introduce you to new levels and new seasons that require you to make adjustments through growth, maturation, and development. Transitions in life are a natural part of life's journey; therefore, expect them. Don't get me wrong; some changes happen without warning, but they need not catch us unprepared. Expected and unexpected life transitions are better handled when you are equipped for them. In this introductory section, I will introduce you to the concept of *NEXTing*. This is where you are encouraged and challenged to understand that now and next meet and collaborate, not collide. Transition should be expected because life, circumstances, situations, and difficult decisions will urge you to transform and transition. Expecting transition is about having a mindset and heart-set that is open to growth, change, and development.

"For I know the plans I have for you," declares the LORD, "plans to prosper you and not to harm you, plans to give you hope and a future."
JEREMIAH 29:11 (NIV)

NEXTing is the conscious anticipation and navigation of the plans of God unfolding in your life as you engage in the now.

The God-created and designed life we receive from Him is not a timid, haphazard life. It's adventurously expectant, greeting God with a childlike "What's next, Papa?" God's Spirit touches our spirits and confirms who we are. We know who He is and who we are: Father and child. And when we trust and believe that God has plans for us, we know we will get what's coming to us—an unbelievable future! We go through exactly what Christ went through, living by faith-navigating and negotiating life transitions. If we go through the complex transitions and times with a Jesus-like attitude, "then we're certainly going to go through the good times with Him!" (Romans 8:15-17, MSG) As you approach every day with an adventurously expectant attitude, you are well on your way to navigating and negotiating life transitions with passion, creativity, and endurance.

"What's Next, Papa?" Beloved, God intends to bring you to an expected end—a future—that is for your good and His glory. Through *"NEXTing,"* by grace through faith, you will arrive at your "next!" "Next" is your future, next level, next assignment, next season, next step, or next opportunity that is a part of God's unfolding plans for you.

It wasn't until I sat down to write this book that I discovered that though change is demanding, natural, and inevitable in life, transition—which is a part of change—is very challenging, thus requiring us to have the capacity and ability to effectively navigate and negotiate transition. According to William Bridges' *Managing Transitions*, transition is the *psychological movement* through the change.[1]

Nearly twenty years ago, my family and I experienced one of the most challenging and crushing changes in our lives: I resigned from my position as pastor of my first church. When I resigned from this pastorate, after serving for a combined ten years, I did not have the skill sets and tools that I have now—the skill sets and tools that I am going to share in the pages of this book. This change shook us to our core and challenged us as a family unit. It wasn't until later in life that I

---

[1] William Bridges, *Managing Transition* (Boston, MA: Da Capo Lifelong Books, 2009).

realized how deeply! Masked—under a zeal and determination to not be undone, disheveled, or defeated—was the deep hurt of this change. The transitions that were a part of this process confirmed to me the need to share this book about *"NEXTing"* with you.

At that time and throughout the process, I, along with my young family, were performing the psychological and emotional gymnastics of a Simone Biles performance but less artistic, graceful, and orderly. I was mentally and emotionally all over the place. Was this change my fault? Had I missed God? Had God abandoned me? Why did I feel blindsided? And if these were the questions that I had, then what of my family? What were my wife and children thinking and feeling? Dad failed! Timothy, what are we going to do now? Change does not happen in a vacuum. When there is change, the impact will be felt by all connected to you.

I felt betrayed by God; if He loved me, then why would He allow me to be blindsided? The institution that was to represent strength and stability for people was now a place of pain and instability. Where was God? What am I going to do? I was devastated and angry at the same time. I was devastated because I felt that I had failed and was of no value anymore. I had let my God down, my wife and children, and the church. I was angry at the church—no—at some of those in the church who had positions of authority and influence and had chosen to wield their authority and influence in a negative manner. So, again, where was God? What was I going to do next?

As I looked into the eyes of my wife and together, we looked at our children, I knew that God had to have a plan! I knew and believed that this change did not catch God off guard, I just was not prepared. All I could think of was the protection and preservation of my family and calling (purpose). So, what was next? What was God up to? What was the next step or turn? Where do I lead my family from here? Man can I tell you that I was scared, unsure, yet hopeful. I was hurting on a deeper level that I didn't know of at the time, too! I was struggling with the internal shame, guilt, and insecurity of the moment of change that was taking place. This was not the changing of a day or a season; this was profound change that I had never experienced before. I had to react, or better yet, I had to respond! No problem can ever be solved on the same level of consciousness that it was created on. Therefore, I knew that God had the answers. I needed His wisdom and guidance. So, I asked God, "What's up?" "What's really going on?" "How are we to get through the change and manage the transitions of change?"

It took nearly twenty years of living and healing until I arrived at the place that I am now. After years of being mad, depressed, ashamed, insecure, and emotionally unhealthy, I can now share with you what God has taught me about that period of my life. God has delivered me from masking my hurt and self-medicating with an undisciplined lifestyle. What I thought was blindsiding was actually the permissive will of God in the unfolding plans of God for my life. "Many are plans in a man's heart, but it is the purposes of God that will and does prevail" (Proverbs 19:21, author paraphrase). A part of my deliverance and healing was the gift of the thoughts and revelations that I will share with you in this book, *NEXTing*.

My worldview informs me that we're an open book to God; even from a distance, God knows what we're thinking. He knows when we leave and when we get back; we're never out of His sight. God knows everything we're going to say before we start the first sentence. We look behind us and He's there, then up ahead, and He's there, too.

> *You know me inside and out; You know every bone in my body; You know exactly how I was made, bit by bit, how I was sculpted from nothing into something. Like an open book, You watched me grow from conception to birth; all the stages of my life was spread out before You, The days of my life all prepared before I'd even lived one day. —Psalm 139, MSG*

Therefore, through His reassuring presence, we do not have to be resigned to aimlessly wandering through life, simply reacting to changes. We can be an active participant in the progressively unfolding plans of God for our lives.

I believe that what God has arranged for us, His Spirit will reveal to us, because "the Spirit is not content to flit around on the surface, but dives into the depths of God, and brings out what God planned all along (1 Corinthians 2, MSG). This way we are not reacting, but we are enabled to respond to the grace of God for what is next efficiently and effectively.

By navigating and negotiating life's transitions, with transformation, I'm realizing that God wants to bring all of us to an expected end (a guaranteed future and hope) filled with brand-new possibilities of change. However, we must learn to navigate and negotiate the land in between (the transitions). To successfully change, you must learn how to manage your transitions. You see, change is simultaneously natural, uncomfortable, and common, but it is the transitions of change that are challenging. They require strategic navigation and negotiation. In this book, you will learn to manage the necessary endings that set us free to look forward to what's next! As you engage in *NEXTing*, you will learn to maximize the new beginnings that open to you, as well as the possibilities of God's future plans for your life, in real-time. *NEXTing* is the key to a better present and a brighter future.

NEXTing is the conscious anticipation and navigation of the plans of God unfolding in your life as you engage in the now.

It is my hope and prayer that, by God's grace through faith—and faith's corresponding actions (hard work and responsibility)—you learn to expect, embrace, and execute your life transitions more skillfully because of *"NEXTing."* You are NEXT! The "NEXT1Up" is you!

Here are a few life transitions we may experience throughout our lives (not an exhaustive list):

1) Grade School Promotions
2) High school to college
3) School to working (or not working)
4) Falling in love to heartbreak
5) Heartbreak to giving love another chance
6) Dating to engaged
7) Single to married
8) Married to divorced or widowed (single again)
9) Life after divorce
10) Getting married again
11) No children to parenting
12) Changing jobs/careers
13) Employed to unemployed
14) Death
15) Moving
16) Becoming empty nesters
17) Adult children returning home
18) Health issues
19) Retirement
20) Taking care of parents

...and the transition you are going through right now!

This book is about *NEXTing*: expecting, embracing, and experiencing transition. *NEXTing* is the effective navigation and negotiation of life transitions of change. *NEXTing is the conscious anticipation and navigation of the plans of God unfolding in your life as you engage in the now.*

1) Expecting Transition
   Transitions in life are a natural part of life's journey; therefore, we should expect them. Don't get me wrong—some changes happen without warning, but they need not catch us unprepared. Expected transitions are better handled when you are equipped for them. Expecting transition is about having a mental attitude, or mindset and heart-set, that is open to growth, change, and development.
2) Embracing Transition
   Whether positive or negative, life transitions cause us to leave behind the familiar and force us to adjust to new ways of living—at least temporarily. Embracing transition will allow you to be an active participant in your progress. When you embrace transition, you are taking ownership of it and the responsibility that comes with that ownership. This sends a message to the transitional moment that you are in—you are not just along for the ride, but you are confident that you can respond appropriately throughout the transition.
3) Experiencing Transition
   There is a difference between existing and living—between surviving and thriving. It is here that we are going to explore how you can live through transition rather than just simply existing while it's happening. We will discuss how you can thrive in change and not merely survive. In committing to experiencing transition, you make the transition work for your growth and development as a person. You move beyond simply having a mental assent to what's happening around you. Experiencing transition will come about because you anticipated it rather than reacted to it.

No matter who you are or where you are, there are events to come in your life. Some of these things will be announced, and some won't be. What's most important to know right now is that there is a "next" in your future. God wants you to live in the now, be present, and remain engaged, all with an anticipation and expectation of the future. He has plans for you that include your prosperity, hope, and future. There are places, ideas, and more postdated for your future that God has ordained, and you must prepare for them in the present. You have an excellent opportunity to make the most of the prized and valued commodity of time by being informed of those plans so that you can be an active participant in your progress as you transition from Now to NEXT.

You have this book in your possession as a tool or resource to help you navigate life's transitions of change. I want to journey with you through your transitions and equip you with tools and tips to help you track through them. I hope to assist you in transitioning into your triumphant NEXT! Navigating and negotiating the expected and unexpected transitions of change in your life is the primary goal of *NEXTing*. Planning for the expected and unexpected is a part of the comprehensive approach of *NEXTing*. Your approach profoundly impacts your transitions, outcomes, and future. What path are you taking? What path will you make in your NEXT change? Are you ready for NEXT? Are you excited about *NEXTing*?

PART I

EXPECTING

*So, beloved, since you are expecting these things,
be eager to be found ... without spot or blemish
and at peace [in serene confidence, free from fears
and agitating passions and moral conflicts].*
2 Peter 3:14, AMPC

CHAPTER 1
NEXTING AS A CONCEPT

Remember this: Anticipation is the ultimate power. Losers react; leaders anticipate.[2]
TONY ROBBINS

NEXTing is the conscious anticipation of the plans of God unfolding in your life as you engage in the now.

Let's explore *NEXTing* as a concept. *NEXTing* is your approach to transition and progress in the flow of your life. It is not the inevitable change of life, nor the accidental growth that takes place in those changes. Rather, *NEXTing* is the mental attitude in which you approach life's transitions. It's about intentionally progressing in the plans and purposes God has for your life. Instead of taking a relatively passive role in transition, *NEXTing* ensures that you're fully engaged and attentively active. When you are *NEXTing*, you see life transitions as part of the plans and purposes for your life. You intentionally

---

2 Tony Robbins, Twitter post, March 21, 2016, 12:38 pm, https://twitter.cpm/TonyRobbins/status/711955140861800448.

participate in those transitions—both the expected and the unexpected. When you are engaged in *NEXTing*, you are moving forward in step with God's purpose towards an expected end.

My first exposure to *NEXTing*, which I didn't recognize at the time, happened on the neighborhood basketball court. In a friend's backyard, the "next" concept was revealed to me. While waiting to play after the current game ended, I was the sole possessor of what we called "next." The next player or team that would play after the game on the court ended had "next." Since I was next, I and a few others stood on the sidelines waiting for the current game to end while preparing for the next, much-anticipated game to start. My game, our game, was next! I was sizing up the competition, huddling to talk strategy, scouting players from either squad currently playing—with my ultimate decision dependent upon who lost. Lo and behold, I was *NEXTing*. You see, the person or team that was preparing to play in the upcoming game was *NEXTing*— strategically navigating and negotiating between the present and the future through mental, physical, and emotional preparation for the next game. I was on the sideline navigating and negotiating the "land in between" or the "time in between" the current game and the next game on the court.

Back in the day, everybody wanted "Next"! Every aspiring basketball player wanted to be in the game. Being in the game meant you had an opportunity to display your skills and even live out some of the dream moves you had practiced in your room with a rolled-up sock and a wastebasket, or a creatively shaped hanger (your breakaway basketball rim) attached to your bedroom door. Being in the game was one of the ways you could silence your critics and be a part of a team that ruled the court for the day. Being in the game meant you were a part of the action and a part of a team. Having "next" opened the door for you to get into the game, where you would either experience the thrill of victory or suffer the agony of defeat ... preferably the former. *NEXTing* is the key that unlocks a different present—and hopefully a brighter future—for the individual or team anticipating the next game.

Being in the game also requires you to confront challenges, be creative, and work hard to succeed. You have removed the fan gear and suited up in the game gear—you are actively involved in the motion and rhythm found on the court. Being in the game means that you are no longer a spectator but a participator! Perhaps that's the way it is in life: you are either a spectator or a participator. I remember one of the rules for getting in the game was that you had to be present. I also remember the anticipation I felt waiting courtside for the current game to end. You had to pay attention and not become distracted because you could miss your turn—or miss a play that revealed a strength (or weakness) of your future opponent (or prospective teammate). There were times when some of us missed our game because we were not paying attention when the current game ended. Sometimes, we had left courtside and were engaged in some other activity. When we missed information that would have benefitted our team, it became evident; we suffered the agony of defeat quite swiftly. Several times, distracted teams missed out on choosing a skillful player who could have helped them win more easily.

While I was waiting and anticipating getting in the game, I had to fight off the distractions of the spectators who had come to check out the competition. I had to disregard the other things vying for my attention, tempting me to miss the moment at hand. We will talk about distractions later in the book. The point I want to make here is that the anticipation of next is as much a part of the game as being *in* the game. Your future directly connects to your present; therefore, you must anticipate and expect it. Anticipation is a verb; it means the action of looking forward to something. It is the visualization of the future. When you are *NEXTing*, you are anticipating what will happen next on

nexting

the court in the next game or in life. ANNOUNCEMENT: YOU'RE THE NEXT-ONE-UP!

Being the next one up or claiming next is that unique place on your life's timeline and the forward-focused mindset and heart-set that connects your present to your future: your Now to your Next. Whenever you decide to declare that you have next, the energy of change begins to flow. The motion of transition is summoned. Remember, victory loves preparation. Therefore, you must prepare for what is coming and what you are about to pursue.

NEXTing is vital because it gives you the opportunity to take it to another level. When you are *NEXTing*, you must be present and paying attention so that you will not miss your turn. You are focused on your current reality because you can learn things that will help you in the future. *NEXTing* requires patience because sometimes, your now is being extended because your next is being prepared. But when your now is ended, it's your turn, to shout, "GOT NEXT!"

The voice of God declares that there is a "next" that is to be expected, embraced, and experienced deep down within us.

NEXTing speaks to the anticipatory nature we possess because a divine sense of eternity has been placed into our hearts by God. It is this anticipation—and its ramifications upon the transitions of life—that I want to explore with you throughout this book. It has been my experience that we are always in some form of transition. We are leaving change, in change, or on our way to change. Change is a constant in life. Life is a series of new beginnings, and with every new beginning, there is an ending. Life is one transition after another; therefore, it is in your best interest to anticipate life's transitions of change skillfully.

WHAT IS TRANSITION?

Transition is movement, passage, or change from one position, state, stage, subject, or concept to another. When we are stagnant, stuck, or have plateaued, frustration can set in because we sense no forward movement or progression in our lives. Stagnation, being stuck, or plateauing can result from us not honestly expecting, embracing, and properly experiencing different transitions in our lives. God does not want you stagnant, stuck, or plateauing. God wants you living and enjoying life to the fullest until it overflows. There is a divine intuition that longs for the announcement of the things that will take place in the future. Within the creative composition of the soul of man lies this anticipatory characteristic, which I refer to as *NEXTing*. The voice of God declares that there is a "next" that is to be expected, embraced, and experienced deep down within us. And if we learn to hear and obey this voice with our inner ear, we will effectively navigate life's transitions. In *NEXTing*, there are people, plans, promises, places, promotions, positions, and prepared positive progress that await you—all of which are consistent with your ordained purpose.

Learning to live in the now—being present and engaging life with anticipation and expectation of the future—is a valuable skill set. It was from the anticipation of waiting for the next game to end and my being the "next one up" back in the day that the idea of *NEXTing* grew its roots. *NEXTing* is more than just a one-word phrase. It is a concept. It includes your approach to what's next in your life. God has plans for you that include your prosperity, hope, and future. There are places, ideas, and so much more postdated for your future that God has ordained, and you must prepare for these things in the present. The divine intuition—the Holy Spirit—within your soul keeps you aware of these plans so that you can be an active participant in your progress as you transition from Now to Next.

NEXTing requires that you expect, embrace, and experience transition. It involves making sure that you do not just hold the anticipated plans and purposes for your life as ideas in your head or sentiments in your heart, but that you work out their implications in every detail of your life (Galatians 5:25-26, MSG, author paraphrase). Friend, the anticipated plans God has for your future can be effectively realized, provided that your approach to those plans is vigilant and progressive.

> **NEXT Notes:** As a creation of God, created on purpose with a purpose, you have purpose in you (good works that you have been appointed to do before the foundation of the world). You need to engage in *NEXTing* because it will help you fulfill your purposed assignment.

NEXTing is believing and taking Jeremiah 29:11 wholeheartedly. The portion of the verse that says "I know the plans that I have for you" reveals that God has thought of you and designed things ahead of time for you. When it comes to God, you are not an afterthought; He has made plans for you to follow, which is the outcome of *NEXTing*. It is believing in this revealed truth and acting upon what you think. You see, faith must have corresponding actions. To say it another way, faith is made evident by your actions. *NEXTing* is incorporating this belief into your approach, your life's strategy, and your goal setting so that you live each day with purpose as those plans are continually unfolding before you. And because you have chosen not to live life as a fan or an involuntary bystander—instead choosing through purposeful living to participate in the progress of the unfolding plans God has for you—you are officially *NEXTing*.

The Bible says in Ephesians 2:10 (AMP):
> *For we are His workmanship [His own masterwork, a work of art], created in Christ Jesus [reborn from above—spiritually*

transformed, renewed, ready to be used] for good works, which God prepared [for us] beforehand [taking paths which He set] so that we would walk in them [living the good life which He prearranged and made ready for us].

Do you believe and receive this truth about your own life? *NEXTing* helps you to appropriate this truth into your approach to life's transitions of change.

> **NEXT Notes:** The voice of God declares that there is a "next" that is to be expected, embraced, and experienced deep down within us. *NEXTing* is the conscious anticipation of the plans of God unfolding in your life as you engage in the now.

NEXTing encourages you to step into the eternal and timeless purpose of God for your life with anticipation and confidence. It calls out to you to identify yourself and prepare for what is to come. *NEXTing* helps to discipline you so that you can keep your priorities in order. It challenges you to examine yourself at the very core of your being so that you are authentic as you transition. *NEXTing* as a concept includes faithfully serving in your now with a confident expectation of the opportunities that await you, because you know and believe that God has plans for you.

Opportunities appear when expectation, preparation, and discipline meet up. God has the plans and has prearranged them for your good; you must be prepared to proceed with them. You must stay alert as you get into position to progress into your plans. There is a direct correlation between managing your now and your capacity to function in what's next.

NEXTing as an approach involves your faithfulness and attention to the now so that you can be better prepared to handle your next. It is a known principle that if you are faithful in the least (now), you will be faithful in the much (next). Therefore, included in the approach of *NEXTing* is a conscious anticipation of the plans God has for you. This anticipation is actualized by being in position to proceed with those plans as they unfold. When you are *NEXTing*, you are not reacting. You are proactively operating because you were anticipating what was to come. *NEXTing* is working with an awareness of your current situation while being forward-looking towards the anticipated plans to prosper you and not to harm you, plans to give you hope and a future! *NEXTing* is a concept of conscious awareness—it is anticipation based upon the plans God has for you that empowers you to be positioned to proceed into those plans. Who's hungry for NEXT?

NEXTing is all about progression: a new thing God has prepared for you. You've got to keep it moving. You can't be afraid to fail. You are in search of mastery and maturation. Your next assignment is right in front of you, and you must prepare for it now. Get ready for NEXT!

Develop *NEXTing* as your approach towards your future. Your next assignment is consistent with your preparation. I am telling you now to get ready for NEXT!

Friend, as you spend time meditating today, listen for that inner voice making announcements and declarations regarding your destiny, which awaits fulfillment. Listen for what must happen and become disciplined in your preparation. It is God who has and knows the best plans for your life, and He calls for you to seek Him. You should not be seeking the plans but seeking the relationship with the One who has and knows the plans. As your relationship with Him grows and develops, the plans will be revealed to you. Many people go after the plans and forsake the relationship with God. It is in Him that we live, move, and have our being; therefore, we should seek after Him. Get to know Him, and you will be at the center of the plans that He has for your life. You may not know the future, but you do know the One who holds the future.

> **You must get in position and work in cooperation with the Spirit if you're going to advance into the plans God has for you.**

NEXTing involves transparency and transformation. You will get to know your authentic self because much of what lies ahead for you is connected to and consistent with what lies within you. *NEXTing* is moving you forward toward your authentic self. You will also discover, as you are *NEXTing*, that you are also transforming. God is a God of change. You will experience profound change at the core of your being that will help you adjust and fit what you are to experience in the future. Beloved, God has plans for you—plans that are tailor-made for you—and He desires that you—the real you—are progressing in those plans.

You must get in position and work in cooperation with the Spirit if you're going to advance into the plans God has for you. Jesus told the disciples to wait in the city until they were endowed with the power to function in their NEXT. The plans God has for you have their root in the spiritual realm. They are comprised of divine intent and the possibility of supernatural manifestation that occurs as you agree with God and trust Him with everything. Hallelujah!

"So, beloved, since you are expecting these things, be eager to be found . . . without spot or blemish and at peace [in serene confidence, free from fears and agitating passions and moral conflicts]" (2 Peter 3:14, AMPC). Do you expect life transitions? Or do you find yourself reacting to what life brings your way?

Transitions are a natural part of life's journey; therefore, we should expect them. Don't get me wrong—some changes happen without warning, but they need not catch us unprepared. Expected transitions are better handled when you are equipped for them. Expecting transition is about having a mental attitude, or mindset and heart-set that is open to growth, change, and development.

What "things" are you to be expecting? Life things. Situations and circumstances that we create by our choices or that may arise because of the intentions of others. Either way, you can choose how you will approach life transitions or respond to them. Peter is encouraging you to be at peace. You can create life transitions, expect them, or respond to them in peace—with serene confidence, free from fears, agitating passions, and moral conflicts through the discipline of *NEXTing*.

Can you imagine moving forward into the plans of God for your life with peace—serene confidence, no fear, free of agitating passions and moral conflicts? What kind of energy would you be putting out into your orbit if you had the peace that comes with expecting God's best for your life? Often what holds us back is the lack of peace that *NEXTing* requires. Surely, when God says, "For I know the plans I have for you,'" declares the LORD, 'plans to prosper you and not to harm you, plans to give you hope and a future'" (Jeremiah 29:11, NIV)—He meant for you to have His perfect peace within you in full operation. Navigating and negotiating life transitions with peace keeps you focused on what's next and from being undone by the unexpected. It is easier to anticipate what is coming when you are in a position of peace. It's easier to make the necessary adjustments when you are in peace. Peace provides the power to consciously anticipate the plans of God unfolding in your life as you engage in the now.

CHAPTER 2
THE DISCOVERY OF *NEXTING*

"He has made everything beautiful and appropriate in its time. He has also planted eternity [a sense of divine purpose] in the human heart [a mysterious longing which nothing under the sun can satisfy, except God]."
ECCLESIASTES 3:11 (AMP)

NEXTing is in your DNA because God placed a sense of divine purpose in your heart. Now it is up to you to discover what that is! It is like a hidden treasure that is worth so much, both now and in the future. Your purpose is your why. And it is definitely a part of the life transitions of change that you have experienced or will experience. The mysterious longing is what helps you fuel the journey that you find yourself on while *NEXTing*. I think that along with the sense of divine purpose and the mysterious longing in our hearts, we were given the emotion of anticipation to help us set out on the journey of discovering, developing, and deploying our purpose as we experience the unfolding plans of God for our lives.

nexting

NEXTing speaks to the anticipatory nature that we possess because a divine sense of eternity has been placed in our hearts by God. I want to explore this anticipation with you and its ramifications upon our transitions in life. It has been my experience that we are always in some form of transition in life. We are leaving change, in change, or on our way to change. Change is a constant. You know that life is a series of new beginnings, and with every new beginning, there is an ending. Life is one transition after another; therefore, anticipating life's changes is in your best interest. But life doesn't just happen, right? Some plans have been made or should be made that connect to your purpose that you may be expecting to happen as you walk out and work out toward your future.

When God placed a divine sense of eternity in your heart, He internally equipped you with GPS (Global Positioning System) hardware in your DNA. WHY? Because God wants to connect you to your destiny. He has divinely created you with the hardware to receive revelation, wisdom, and guidance from above, so you do not have to lean or rely on your understanding, but you can trust Him, and He will direct your path (Proverbs 3:5-6, author paraphrase). God has made you this way so you can connect purpose with His plans, meaning to the moments, significance to steps, direction to dreams, value to vision, and hope to what's on the horizon.

You can dream and see visions of a better present and a brighter future because of the eternity in you. God believes in you and cares for you to trust you with such valuable information that creates a longing in you for the manifestation of His plans for your life. You find yourself thinking about what life is and what life could be. You dream of what is and is yet to be created or invented. You see opportunities where there are challenges.

The blessing of being able to receive heavenly downloads and be wired for eternal revelation and information comes with the responsibility of stewardship. God hopes and expects you to be faithful. To be a faithful steward of the planted eternity in your heart is to trust and obey God.

As a faithful steward of continual heavenly deposits, your progress moves at the speed of trust.

You must trust that God knows and wants the best for you. Put your trust in God's love for you and that He created you purposefully. Trusting God is feeling careless, confident, and content in His character. When you trust God, you are not concerned or worried that His love and grace won't be enough. And you are not concerned or worried that every detail of your life is continually woven together for good, for you are His lover who has been called to fulfill His designed purpose (Romans 8:28, author paraphrase). When you trust God, you trust the timing of God too. "He has made everything beautiful and appropriate in its time" (Ecclesiastes 3:11, AMP). As a faithful steward of continual heavenly deposits, your progress moves at the speed of trust.

The speed of trust. Do you believe that God has a plan for your life? And do you trust Him to reveal that plan to you over time throughout life's journey? A lack of trust in the love and power of God will undermine your discovery or His revealing of the plans that He has for you. Trust speaks to your heart and your head. In your thoughts and feelings, where are you when it comes to trusting that God wants the best for you? You must trust God even when the transition is painful that there is a greater purpose in His permissive will for your life. When you are uncomfortable with the current conditions of a transition, your trust in God will help you become comfortable with being uncomfortable, and you will begin to make adjustments rather than complain or quit in the middle of transitions.

Another aspect of stewarding the divine sense of purpose given to you by God is obedience. You must do what He tells you, nothing more and nothing less. The plans that God has for you come with instructions that are expected to be followed by you. When you are *NEXTing*, God wants you to follow the turn-by-turn directions that He provides as the route He selected for you unfolds. We will discuss this later but now, know that obedience is easier when you trust the source providing the instruction and guidance. I must laugh at myself here because I am reminded of the many times that I have hesitated or stopped in the middle of the route selected by my GPS because in my mind, I knew a different way or felt like the AI got it wrong. To keep it simple, I don't trust the AI, operate in disobedience, and then complain when I get lost! So, trust and obedience go hand in hand in the discovery of *NEXTing*.

Bringing out the best in you often means letting go of the familiar and worst in you.

In the discovery of *NEXTing*, a transformation of the soul often accompanies the life transitions of change. God wants to bring all of us to an expected end (a guaranteed future and hope) filled with new possibilities. To see and experience the new possibilities on the other side of the transition of change, you must become new from the inside out. Bringing out the best in you often means letting go of the familiar and worst in you. As you are navigating the transition of change, there is going to be change in you. Your thoughts, your emotions, and even your will are impacted by the transition. I can guarantee that you will not be the same person coming through the transition or out of the change. A part of the discovery of *NEXTing* is discovering you, the real you. When you are *NEXTing*, you are discovering the layers that must be peeled back so that you can be authentically you. You will be brought face to face with the pain of change and growth. You will discover as I did that to do better you have to be better! You must show God where it hurts. I am reminded of Mary and Martha in the Bible when they were expressing their frustration about the timing of Jesus' arrival after they sent news of their brother Lazarus' sickness. Jesus says to Mary at one point in the discourse, "Where have you put him?" (John 11:34, NLT) Confronting the hurt places and dead places is a part of your transformation in the discovery of *NEXTing*.

From the place of vulnerability, discovery is necessary for there to be transformation through the transition of change. You learn of the presence of God as your assistant who navigates and negotiates the land in between. To successfully transition, you must learn to manage your exits and maximize your entrances. The exits you will learn to work on are the necessary endings that set you free and prepare you for what's next. The entrances you will learn to maximize are the new beginnings that open the possibilities of "next" in real-time.

Knowing and believing that the *NEXTing* DNA is in you will help you when you feel stuck. Have you ever realized that you were living your life on autopilot? It's literally like you put your life on cruise control! You recognize that you have decades of experience in a particular area and you're doing pretty good, but then something in your life happens, and you believe that that good is just not good enough! You have that "ah-ha" moment! At one time or another, every person loses momentum, plateaus, and feels stuck in the mud. When this happens, what do you do? I'm glad you asked! You need to remember that you have the *NEXTing* DNA inside of you.

What if you were created to be more? What if you were designed for excellence? What if you were created to go to the next level in your life, leadership, and business? What if that was possible? I am here to tell you that it is! I was that dude, after building a successful career for thirty years in my industry and achieving a doctorate degree in my field, I had put my life on autopilot. I put my career on cruise control. I was coasting. And I will be transparent with you—I was stuck and didn't know it! I had resigned my life to doing just enough to get by and retire. Inertia had begun to set up in my heart and mind because there was a disconnect between me and my purpose. BUT, SOMETHING HAPPENED that challenged and helped to change me. I attended a conference that compelled me to make a change. Sometimes you must get in a different room to have a different perspective, the *NEXTing* perspective. I got in the right room, the room where it happens—and the room that I am talking about is not measured by square footage. No, it is not 60 ft by 60 ft! The room was my head/heart! The right room is your head/heart! The room where it happens is your head/heart! Your thinking/feelings! I remembered what Ecclesiastes 3:11 (AMP) says, "He has made everything beautiful and appropriate in its time. He has also planted eternity [a sense of divine purpose] in the human heart [a mysterious longing which nothing under the sun can satisfy, except God]."

Sometimes you have to bet on yourself. You must invest in yourself! Your best life can be what's next! It's in you! It is in your DNA! Your next is in the "right room" of your head/heart! And today as you are reading, you're in the right room too! Please close your eyes for a minute, and I want you to think about where you are in your life right now and where you want to be, and know that it's possible for you! I know you're excited right now; I know you're fired up; I know you want to get to what's next! Can I give you the triple A strategy on how you can have the *NEXTing* perspective? Do I have your permission to share the Triple A strategy with you? Now, you can apply this to your leadership; you can apply this to your life; but really, I just want you to apply this to your purpose!

1) Awareness: Awareness is the catalyst for all meaningful change in your life! There are two types of awareness: internal self-awareness (how you see yourself matters, your values, your beliefs, passions, strengths, stretch points, your boundaries, your go-lines, and your why?) and external self-awareness (how others see you—what is it like being on the other side of you?)
2) Access: Access point is all about CONNECTION—people, relationships, resources, ideas, capital, and opportunities that you expose yourself to. Access works both ways. As opportunities and resources open their doors to you, YOU MUST AT THE SAME TIME THROW OPEN YOUR DOORS! YOU MUST BE ACCESSIBLE! APPROACHABLE! CONNECTABLE! What vibe are you sending to people? Are you engaging? Do you want to make connections?

The reality is that you can have an awareness of who you are, and you can be accessible, but at the end of the day, if you don't act, your life is not going to look any different!

3) Action: You've got to take action in your life so you can be the person you were created to be, make full use of the resources within and around you, and get to your next! I need you to commit to LIVING IN COMMITTED ACTION. Adopt the *NEXTing* perspective and adapt to the process! I like using the root word of action, A.C.T., as an acronym.

Action Conquers Timidity. Don't allow fear to keep you trapped! Fear will imprison you in your thinking, creating strongholds that hold you back! It's time for a breakout! It's time to ACT and start breaking down your walls of fear.

Action Changes Things. Delays in action or failure to move at all will net the same results; nothing will change. But when you commit to taking action and commit to what Joe Navarro calls "movement to action", you will change things and generate a positive response on the other end of your actions. This is why the renowned Ritz-Carlton leadership training course emphasizes taking action as soon as possible!

Action Claims Territory. It's time for your feet to tread on some new ground. Your territory has been enlarged; now go get it! Take the first step to claim the territory that you have the title deed to! It's yours but you've got to go get it!

As we navigate through life, some moments define our purpose and remind us why we do what we do. The triple A strategy (Awareness, Access, Action) is designed to work together to produce the *NEXTing* perspective needed for powerful change in your life. Just because the job is getting done doesn't mean you're flourishing. It's time that you SHIFT OUT OF CRUISE CONTROL, SHUT DOWN AUTOPILOT, AND GO FROM EXISTING TO LIVING! TO GO FROM NOW TO NEXT! It's in your DNA; you were designed to live an amazing life, to be and do extraordinary work, and to make a bigger impact.

As you discover *NEXTing* within you, you are shaking off the oppressive mindset and heart-set and casting down the strongholds that reduce you to a shadow of existence. It's your eleventh hour. Make a supreme decision and effort to turn the page and start a new chapter in your leadership and lifework! When you elevate the way you think and feel about life, the life you live will become different! Say this with me, "It's my time and it's my turn! Next is Now! And I am the "NEXT1UP!"

The discovery of *NEXTing* also involves the *NEXTing* mindset and heart-set, which suggests that whatever you long for and expect in the future inevitably determines how you live in the present. Hope, and its desires, are the engine that drives you. Pursuing a greater good in the future is the sole motive strong enough to bring about a willing and persevering self-denial in the present. Only the confident expectation of a future interest can outweigh the burdens you are currently experiencing in your world. One of the keys to the *NEXTing* mindset and heart-set is having a vision of the future: where you want to be next.

This vision will help to qualify your decisions in the present and build your confidence in your future.

When your past isn't behind you, it's difficult to anticipate what's next or what could be.

Discovering *NEXTing* showed me that without confidence in your future and a growing longing for what could be, your perseverance will be undermined by past and present challenges. When you are going through the life transitions of change, you are challenged to endure and operate with consistency. You must develop a short-term memory; you cannot dwell on defeat, failure, and setbacks for a long time. You must learn how to get back up when you get knocked down and keep it moving. Your confidence in your future will feed your hopes and your hopes determine your habits. You have been made for a brighter future designed by God; therefore, you are a future-determined person. Your future should dictate your level of determination and steadfastness during challenging times. To avoid losing heart now, a vision of what's next must captivate your mind and heart.

The vision that comes with *NEXTing* helps to move your past to where it needs to be ... behind you! When your past isn't behind you, it is hard to visualize a better present and a brighter future! The past clouds your view and crowds your mind and heart, thus immobilizing you or worse, pushing you in the wrong direction—backward. When your past isn't behind you, it's difficult to anticipate what's next or what could be. A past that is out of place creates anticipatory anxiety. When you should be looking for what's next, you are too busy worrying about what was and how you cannot move on and move forward. Stuck or moving in the wrong direction is the result of your mind and heart being out of sync with the open door of opportunity that is before you, even if that open door is beyond a very challenging and hurtful transition. The vision that comes with *NEXTing* puts the past behind you and your future in front of you. When the vision of your future is in front of you, you will be able to endure as you press toward the mark of what is NEXT!

Vision gives you a "*NEXTing* perspective," which is an elevated perspective. When you are *NEXTing*, you get a different reference point because of the elevated perspective. The elevated perspective is God's viewpoint, His thoughts, and His ways regarding your life, your life experiences, and this world. It is His way of seeing matters that pertain to life and godliness in the world in which we live.

The discovery of this perspective provides you with a different reference point so that you can live your life and operate according to a next-level dimension! A reference point (also point/frame of reference) is an idea, fact, event, etc. that you already know, which helps you understand or make a judgment about another situation. A point of reference helps you discern a situation or communicate with someone. A next-level reference point will enable you to make godly decisions and choices.

When you have the *NEXTing* perspective as your reference point, you will subconsciously evaluate what's next for your life from the vision of the plans that God has for you, which was ordained by God.

Have you ever met somebody who is always negative, always pessimistic? They are Captain Negative, with the nickname Negative Nelly. Draining, Drama, and Dreary! They never have anything positive to say! Forever complaining! This is not right; this is too cold! It's too hot! I'll never make it! I'll never get ahead! Why do bad things always happen to me? Well, if you have met this person—and I'm pretty sure you have—you must wonder and question, what is their point of reference? Whose perspective do they have? What idea, what facts are they using to help them to make this judgment about their lives, their life situations, and their future? What point of reference are they referring to communicate this dreary forecast about life? I bet you it is the natural! Or their family's socialization or their life's conditioning by the world around them. You and I both know that the reference point did not come from an elevated *NEXTing* perspective. The vision that comes from *NEXTing* encourages you to feast on the brighter future from the plans of God and fill your thoughts with heavenly realities, and not with the distractions of the natural realm.

The vision that comes from *NEXTing* helps to give you a better perspective of your present (your now) and your future (your next). Perspective is everything! With a fresh perspective that comes from *NEXTing*, you see clearer what is going on in your present (your now), and you are better positioned to imagine a brighter next (future). The "*NEXTing* perspective" provides you with a vantage point that recenters you so you will know how far you have come and how far you must go to arrive at your next destination! It is vital to be able to recenter yourself before moving forward. Vision does that. Vision directs you to what is important and where you are headed. Oftentimes life's transitions come with distractions, detours, and delays that can throw you off spiritually, mentally, emotionally, physically, socially, or financially. When and if this happens, the *NEXTing* perspective of vision helps to inwardly reset your compass and redirect your energy and efforts towards that which is productive and beneficial to where you are going. I talk about this more in my sequel to this book, *Lost in Transition*.

> **NEXT Notes:** Remember the discovery of *NEXTing* comes from the divine sense of purpose that has been planted in your heart, which gives birth to vision and sound.

CHAPTER 3
NEXTING HAS A VOICE

"Then I looked, and, oh!—a door open into Heaven. The trumpet-voice, the first voice in my vision, called out, 'Ascend and enter. I'll show you what happens next.'"
REVELATION 4:1 (MSG)

NEXTing can be likened to responding to the voice of a navigational system with intentional and deliberate actions, motions, and turns. Once you input your destination, then the audible AI voice provides you with turn-by-turn guidance to assist in your navigation to arrive at your destination. In other words, your next has a voice. The inner voice that you are hearing now about your tomorrow and your future functions as a call and an exhortation. Your next will talk to you; it will call out to you; it will encourage you; it will be a voice deep within that you sometimes hear softly like a whisper or loudly like thunder. It will speak consistently and firmly until you respond. In the discovery of *NEXTing*, the voice of next speaks to the connection that you have with your next. Remember your next has been downloaded into your heart, into your DNA! You have a divine sense of purpose within you! And the voice of next speaks to that designed purpose within you. It will speak according to the desires of your heart and the purposes of God for your life. And, at other times, it will announce upcoming detours or changes. The voice of next is connected to the vision of your future. The voice gives instructions and information. The voice announces the open door of opportunity that is before you, even when the open door of opportunity is disguised as a challenge or problem. Do you hear it? Are you listening? The Voice of Next is calling out to you!

> **NEXT Notes:** When the winning team on the court yells out, "Who's got next?" This can be likened to the voice of next calling out to you, too, alerting you to the opportunities that are before you. Your future is calling. Do you hear it? Do you have next?

At this point, it is important to know how to distinguish the voice of your next from all the other voices calling out to you externally and internally. External voices (noise) exist all around us in the form of things like traffic, television, cell phones, politicians, and critics. These external voices can become deafening to the voice of your next if you are not careful with noise canceling and volume control. The ears of your head and heart must be sensitive to the lies of the enemy because he wants you constantly listening to the toxic, destiny-stealing, and destroying sounds of his rhetoric in whatever voice he can disguise it. Next, you must pay attention to the internal voices in the form of constant thoughts. We don't often think of the noise in our heads, but more and more of us are beginning to believe that our internal thoughts (the noise in our heads/hearts) might be complicating life and stressing us out. These voices could include worry, anger, fear, anxiety, and lies that we tell ourselves. *NEXTing* encourages you to be intentional about identifying the distinct and unique frequency of the voice of your next. Its tone and tenor should be identifiable not only in sound but also in content. The sound of your next cannot be fabricated or duplicated. You must honor your sound sensitivity. Identify voice imitators, sound-offenders, and noisemakers, and develop healthy boundaries and a plan that serves you, like noise-blocking earbuds. Whenever the voice of my next is threatened or is starting to blend in with the other voices, I use reading, meditation, exercise, praying, golfing, listening to audiobooks/messages, and outdoor cycling to help me hear clearly again.

The voice of next calls out from the future vision that is higher than your current position and further than your present location.

The voice of next calls out from the future vision that is higher than your current position and further than your present location. Yes, what you are hearing is calling out from where you are headed. Sometimes the voice tells you that you must come up higher and level up because where you are is not where you are meant to be! The voice declares that you must change and elevate your position so that you can receive and possess a higher perspective on what is next for you. Simultaneously, the voice is beckoning you to keep going forward and beyond where you are now so that you can experience what is next. The voice becomes a driving force within your mind and heart.

I remember the voice of my next when I finally decided to announce my resignation from my first pastorate in November, 2000. The voice started out as a whisper nine months before while I was attending a conference about change in Atlanta, GA, in February, 2000. I kept hearing something in my spirit that I tried to make sense of in my soul. The voice kept announcing to me, "Change is coming in your life and ministry!" The voice penetrated my being and impregnated my mind and heart. The voice of my next was talking to me consistently over the next nine months as it grew clearer. Communication fosters clarity and clarity provokes action! I said—communication fosters clarity and clarity provokes action. The voice of my next became a driving force in my life.

> **NEXT Notes:** I decree that the voice of your next becomes a driving force of your destiny!

The voice of your next is the driving force of an inner voice urging you to keep going no matter what! It will be of great value, especially when you respond and act. Why? Because others will not hear what you hear. And because of their ignorance, they may judge you and become critical and condemning of your actions. Others who may not understand your why, what, how, who, when, and where will start to question your life transition. You are going to need to know that what you heard was from the voice of your next and not multiple voices around you from others. More often than not, the majority will not agree with you about what your next should be, but that should not matter to you when the driving force of exhortation is turned on and the volume is turned up! Others present with you may want to offer their voice of reason and discouragement—to try to convince you to go in the direction of their choosing. But remember, in *NEXTing*, you are pursuing the plans God has for you; therefore, His voice of exhortation must become the loudest voice in the room to you. In the discovery of *NEXTing*, the driving force of God's persuasion will move you towards change and growth when others don't hear it, understand it, or agree with it.

Warning: do not share with others what you are hearing until you are clear about what you are hearing.

Have you discovered the voice of your next? Have you heard the voice of your next calling out to you? The voice will speak to you in your language; the voice will talk to you at a level that you can understand. The voice is a confirming and affirming word from your next. Sometimes, the voice of your next is echoed by those whom God places in your life, and sometimes it's not. That should not matter if you have ears to hear what God is saying to you. You must be tuned into the right frequency through prayer and meditation. I encourage you to quiet yourself before the Father so that you may hear His voice clearly so as not to follow some other voice that is speaking around you and even sometimes within you. Please, pause and really listen to me here, because your next is of value to me. It is important that you understand and apply this principle. Communication fosters clarity! I remember when I heard the voice of my next calling out to me to elevate and progress and began to share a little of what I heard with others. I opened the door for them to give me their unsolicited opinion. BIG MISTAKE! Warning: do not share with others what you are hearing until you are clear about what you are hearing. When the voice of your next becomes a vision to you that your heart and mind receive and perceive, you then can write it down and make it plain (discuss it with others). Be prepared for feedback that may contradict what you heard and are hearing. Once the voice becomes a vision that speaks and does not lie, then you have clarity and are ready to act!

The voice is an invitation to another dimension of living. The voice of next will function as a shepherd—leading and guiding, protecting and correcting, and disciplining you. The voice motivates you to fulfill the purpose of your next. The voice of next calls out and raises its volume when necessary. The voice of your next encourages you to blend your voice with it, creating one voice that speaks securely and loudly.

The driving force of exhortation encourages your voice in the transitions of life. It is time to believe and speak! It is time to dream and declare! It is time to receive revelation and release your faith into the atmosphere by your confession and decree! Do not allow the enemy, hurt, surprise, or negativity—or life—to silence you any longer! Do not allow your current condition to become your conclusion. Open your mouth and shout, right now, "TO BE CONTINUED!" Do not let what appears to be a delay turn into discouragement and give voice to doubt and disbelief. Next has a voice! Did you hear what I said? Next without a voice is a dead end! What do you do when the voice of the GPS in your car does not announce the next turn or next direction? You keep driving in the direction of the last instruction. In other words, you keep moving unless you see that what is ahead is a dead end.

The driving force of exhortation wants you to speak up and out—to declare what that voice is saying—to the life event, crisis, or circumstances in front of you. SAY SOMETHING! SAY SO! You have the driving force of exhortation living in you, breathing in you, stirring in you, growing in you. What kind of driving force? The type that BELIEVES AND THEREFORE SPEAKS! STAND UP AND SPEAK UP AND SAY WHAT YOU BELIEVE!

Place a premium on the driving force of exhortation speaking within you. Make a point to speak what it says out loud. Stop allowing people to discount either of these speaking opportunities. Everyone has an opinion about your next, some will just think it, and others will be bold enough to share it with you. Fret not, what is vital at this transitional moment in your life is what you hear within and what you speak!

The driving force of the voice of next is divine promptings from within. Through prayer and meditation, remarkable secrets about things to come can be revealed to you so that you can effectively navigate life's transitions of change. Divine secrets are revelations that God keeps hidden and only shows to those intended to benefit. These secrets contain information that, if disclosed before authorized, would endanger divine destiny and purpose. The devil and his demons (fallen angels) do not want you as a believer to know the divine secrets. But God in His infinite wisdom and divine timing has decided to reveal them to those who love Him.

The driving force of exhortation is being established in your hearing today as you read this book. The voice of your next is calling out to you! Tune in to His frequency if you want to excel in this place of change and growth. When the haters of this world seek to discourage you, you may need to reduce and even eliminate that noise so that His voice of wisdom is the only one that you hear as it urges you to come up and carry on to your next!

CHAPTER 4
THIS CAN'T BE HAPPENING

Sometimes life takes an unexpected wrong turn in the right direction.
Chris Thompson

In a State Farm TV commercial of 2016, the phrase, *"this can't be happening,"* is uttered by a man who is walking towards his car on a cell phone only to see that his car has been jacked up sitting on cement blocks with tires stolen, front bumper gone, and windows broken out. He screams and utters the words, *"This can't be happening, what a day!"* Another voice says, *"Oh, this is happening!"* Then there is the voice of the State Farm agent in a calming voice that says, *"That's why State Farm is there offering car insurance for when life goes wrong to help things go right."*

How prepared are you for when *"this can't be happening,"* is happening to you or around you? How prepared are you for when the unexpected happens? I recall a time when I was waiting courtside for the current basketball game to end and the next to begin. There were only five of us waiting at the time, and a team is five players, so I was confident that I would be on the next team taking the court. I was anticipating getting in the game so I could show off my moves and have some fun. In the current game, it was game point—only one more basket and it would be over! As soon as the game was over, another player showed up, and he was chosen over me! Fair? Yes. But totally unexpected!

I was blindsided! This can't be happening, right? But it was. What I did not expect and did not want was happening. How was I to react or respond? What had it done to my confidence? Should I wait around for the next game or not? When you are *NEXTing* you learn to pause, catch your breath, and reassess things before responding. So, I adjusted my attitude and focused on why I was there and what I was going to do next. It's not over when you lose or don't get picked—it is over when you quit! I was disappointed about not getting picked but I was not going to quit! I had come out to play basketball that day and I kept my focus on that. And I was going to play because now, I was next! I remained focused while preparing for the game to end. "Sometimes life takes an unexpected wrong turn in the right direction." During the game, a player on the winning team had to leave and because I was present, focused, and prepared for next—I was picked up by the winning team to fill the exiting player's spot. And we ran the court the rest of the day (four winning games straight)! Can you say "dynasty?" What was a blindside turned out to be an unexpected wrong turn in the right direction for me that day.

Have you ever been blindsided? Has the unexpected and unwanted ever happened to you? I'm sure it has. How well did you fare? While it is illogical to expect that we'll anticipate every possible scenario, it is possible to be mentally and emotionally prepared for life's unexpected transitions through *NEXTing*. When the unexpected is happening, don't panic, H.A.L.T., and breathe!

H.A.L.T. stands for hold up, assess the situation, look within, and take authority. H.A.L.T. allows you to breathe. Halting and breathing prevent us from panicking and eliciting a knee-jerk reaction. As we are practicing H.A.L.T., we get to breathe, which nourishes our physical body by oxygenating our cells, promoting healing, and boosting our immune system. Simultaneously, it calms our minds, quieting the incessant chatter and allowing us to tap into a state of deep relaxation and peace. This combination of halting and breathing is a process that helps you to navigate and negotiate your next move from a position of self-control in the middle of unexpected wrong turns in the right direction.

The blindside can be a fact, but it only disturbs us insofar as it resonates with our own emotional turmoil.

NEXTing helped me appreciate that sometimes life takes wrong turns in the right direction after I learned the value of self-awareness. Is the blindside happening to you or around you? Why are you thinking and feeling the way that you are? Why are you reacting or responding in the way that you are? The blindside or the *"thing that can't be happening"* but is could be a test of your mental fortitude. The blindside can be a fact, but it only disturbs us insofar as it resonates with our own emotional turmoil. If our mind is still and our hearts are calm, no unexpected event can unsettle or dishevel us and throw us into an out-of-control spiral, but if our minds and hearts are anxious, fearful, or full of insecurity and low self-esteem, the road ahead will be rocky, and your reaction or response will reflect that.

You must learn to reach a state of rest and peace within so that the blindside or the unexpected does not have a devastating effect upon you and your future. For when you have sincerely quieted your soul and have restrained the outward forces' power to intimidate you, then no outward thing will move you to stressful levels; no actions of men or

52 nex**ting**

drama without can interrupt your peace and rest when you have become steadfast and sure. The soul that reacts to events or chance happenings is unstable and has not yet withdrawn into itself; it contains within itself an element of anxiety and rooted fear, and this makes one prey to chance and forever a victim of blindsides. You may therefore be sure that you are at peace with yourself when no blindside cancels you or when no unexpected drama shakes you out of yourself. When I felt blindsided by the events that led to my resigning from my first pastorate, I found it very helpful to ask myself, "Does my annoyance have more to do with me or my prejudices than with the events themselves?" Was my extreme discomfort and instability due to me not anticipating what was next and being unprepared for my future than what was happening in real-time?

NEXTing through unexpected transitions of life amid change is possible as you settle yourself and possess your thoughts, emotions, and options for what is next by halting and breathing. Let's break it down and see what this looks like in the State Farm commercial scenario. When the unexpected is happening, what do you do? You—H.A.L.T.! Once you acknowledge that the unexpected is happening, you go into H.A.L.T. mode.

H: Holding Up (while breathing) is where you don't move or react in haste, but you slow things down mentally and emotionally. Holding Up is pausing so you can gather your faculties after being blindsided by the unexpected.

A: Assess the Situation (while breathing). Gather information, separating facts from fiction and opinions. Is it happening to you or around you? You also assess the impact of the blindside by taking inventory (what's lost, gained, changed, etc.).

L: Look within (while breathing) instead of at what you can't believe is happening. Your power lies within and not in what is happening to you or around you externally. The presence of God, peace, wisdom, and strength is going to come from within you. So often we struggle to move forward to our next because we have given our power to the external event that is happening either to us or around us. Looking within (while breathing) is how you maintain your power and authority so you can explore the options that you have to choose from.

T: Take authority (while breathing). This is where you exercise your free will and make a decision. What's your response to the life transition of change that you are experiencing? When you make your H.A.L.T. and breathing a priority each day of your life, you make dealing with unexpected life transitions more manageable. H.A.L.T. can become a daily meditation time discipline that will help provide balance. In *NEXTing* for the unexpected, consistent H.A.L.T. and breathing are the best anticipatory preparations you can have to ensure growth and development, no matter what you have to face.

As I reflect on my growth and development as a person through the different blindsides I've encountered, it was and is halting and breathing that have helped me to effectively navigate and negotiate life transitions of change. I like to say to myself, *"blindsided, but I'm breathing!"*

The Bible tells us in Philippians 4:6 (AMP), "Do not be anxious or worried about anything, but in everything [every circumstance and situation] by prayer and petition with thanksgiving, continue to make your [specific] requests known to God." Halting and breathing can be enveloped in the prayers and petitions with thanksgiving that you make to God about what is happening in your life.

This can't be happening, but it is! And it is okay, and it is going to be okay because you are *NEXTing*! You are learning to navigate and negotiate your way to your next! Don't forget to H.A.L.T., if you must.

NEXT Notes: Halting is breathing through what is happening on your way to your next. Halting is breathing through the noise.

CHAPTER 5
WHAT HAPPENS NEXT IS VERY IMPORTANT

"Faith is anticipation minus anxiety."[3]
STEVEN FURTICK

As you are still in discovery mode of *NEXTing*, it is vital that you believe that God does have plans for you and that you believe in those plans and the future that He has for you. Often, we go backwards, get stuck, or don't move forward because of the lack of belief that the future is possible. Believing that you have a future encourages you to hope and not to worry at the intersection of life transitions of change and faith. Your future is what has not yet happened but you believe exists. What has not yet happened is of value to you. Let nothing and no one reduce its value in your life. *NEXTing* requires faith. And as Steven Furtick says, "Faith is anticipation minus anxiety."

---

3   Steven Furtick, Twitter post, June 28, 2016, 9:01 pm, https://twitter.com/stevenfurtick/status/747958215682441216.

NEXTing involves anticipating without stressing over the unknown. *NEXTing* involves anticipating without fearing the unknown. You can anticipate your next without stress or fear because of your belief that your next is a part of the plans that God has for you. Because you believe that God values you enough that He has thought of plans to prosper you and to give you a future and expected end, you should believe that the plans are of value, too. Therefore, if it is of God, why should you have stress or fear? When you anticipate life's transitions of change, you will need to adapt an attitude that says, "What comes next is very important." This attitude will serve you well as you understand that what you are taking on—whether expected or unexpected—has purposeful and redemptive significance for your future self. The act of expecting in *NEXTing* is described as an attitude of bold and courageous anticipation—minus the anxiety and fear. Expecting life's transitions in *NEXTing* means that you open yourself up to a world full of possibilities, wonder, and deeper connection. You don't have to run away from life your entire life. You can live differently because you choose to believe that what happens next is of value and not some haphazard event or change.

God has either intentionally moved in your life or permissively allowed a life transition of change to initiate a next—a total life-change—for your transformation and transition. Your next is according to the plans He has for you. It involves a process of change and motion. It is connected to the purpose He has designed for your life. It will be meaningful and powerful. Its value should be appreciated and anticipated without anxiety and the torment of fear.

Beloved, you are loved by God who has thought of you before the foundations of the earth and has made plans and purposed those plans to be fulfilled in your life. Now surrender and trust Him! By grace through faith believe that the best is yet to come! What happens next is very important because it is a part of the plans and process that God is working out in you and through your life. Right now, at this discovery moment in your life, surrender it all to the Father—your joys and sorrows, hopes and fears, goals and disappointments. Don't hold anything back. By faith, stand boldly in the grace wherein you stand and release control of those parts of your life that you've held on to. *NEXTing* is navigating and negotiating without stressing about the turns and adjustments that you must make. Your next is in front of you so surrender to God any pain, fear, trust issues, bad habits, wrong attitudes, or areas of your life that are holding you back. When you release these to the Father, you are releasing the anxiety that accompanies them so that you can move forward into your next. *NEXTing* is surrendering what you think you can control or what you want to control over to God and submitting to His plans for your life.

Find your delight and true pleasure in Yahweh, and he will give you what you desire the most. Give God the right to direct your life, and as you trust Him along the way, you'll find He pulled it off perfectly. —Psalm 37:5 (TPT)

The plans may be totally life-changing in a specific area of your life. Whatever it is, you can anticipate without anxiety because you believe in the built-in value that the plans of God have. Friend, no matter what you have been told up to now about your life and where you are, I want you to know that you are of value and what God has planned for your future is of value too! Allow this thought to quicken or make alive the hope and confidence that you have in God and His plans for your life. It is possible to grow—to become who you want to be. It is possible to change and be changed because of the value-added benefit of knowing that the plans of God will succeed. Hidden in your *NEXTing* is change. Yes, it will be significant, influential, and even intimidating; but trust God, believing that He has your best interest at heart. Don't allow fear or the past to rob you of your next. Change is awaiting you just around the corner.

nexting

Anticipate the future, bury the past, and keep it moving, because your next is now: you have things to do and places to go!

NEXTing encourages you to anticipate what happens next. Your heightened spirit within is a motivating presence and power that encourages and enables you to become bold and courageous in the face of challenging circumstances and life events. It attracts energy and summons inner power within so that you can become creative and innovative in preparation for what is about to happen in your life.

Anticipate the future, bury the past, and keep it moving, because your next is now: you have things to do and places to go! Through the grace of God, refocus your attention on what lies ahead. Don't focus on what has happened in your past. Why? Because it is important!

> ***NEXT Notes:*** Far too often, we miss out on what God is doing now and what He wants to reveal to us about our future because we are stuck in reverse. You need to engage in *NEXTing* because it will help you get unstuck.

The past can hold us hostage, preventing us from expecting or being hopeful about our present and our future. The past does not have to be negative to hold us back, either; past successes can be just as immobilizing as failures. Successes can be misleading and deceptive, providing a premature finish or sense of arrival. However, when kept in the proper perspective, successes indicate progress in the right direction. Likewise, failures are discoveries that we may be headed in the wrong direction or that we need to move forward with a different approach. Either way, move beyond your past because God sees you beyond your past.

He sees you as you are and as you can become. *NEXTing* is calling you forward. You have work to do. There is so much more that God wants to do in and through you. Move into your next with confidence and expectancy, knowing you are loved by God and knowing who you are in relation to Him. *NEXTing* moves from expecting transition to embracing transition.

An essential part of embracing transition is the exit. Exits are necessary endings that set us free for what is next. Accepting the end of something is critical to establishing the beginning of something else. Too often, next is forfeited because an exit is poorly executed. An exit must be embraced in several areas of one's being. To embrace the exit physically but not mentally can prove to be harmful because it is incomplete. A whole and complete ending creates the foundation for a new beginning.

> ***NEXT Notes:*** Events and experiences poorly processed can prove to be problematic for future endeavors. ***NEXTing*** will help you to properly process previous and present life events.

WHAT COMES NEXT

In this time of your life, you will need to adopt an attitude that says, "What comes next is very important." You must place a value on your future! Say to yourself, *"My future is important to me; it has value!"* This attitude will serve you well as you begin to prepare for this great undertaking called transition—whether expected or unexpected. Either way, it has purposeful and redemptive significance for your future self. The act of anticipating in *NEXTing* can be described as an attitude of bold and courageous expectations—minus anxiety and fear. Expecting life's transitions in *NEXTing* means that you open yourself up to a world full of possibilities, wonder, and deep connection. You don't have to run away from life your entire life. You can live differently because you can change, adjust to change, and be an agent of change.

Friend, place a high value on what you are gaining and not what you are losing.

Yes, your future is of tremendous value and no price can be placed on it. Think about it, what could the world possibly offer you for your secure, planned, hopeful, and divinely designed tomorrow, called next? Nothing! Absolutely nothing! Keep this in mind as you prepare to go through the process of transition: the trade-off of your now for your next often comes with pain and discomfort, but it is worth it. Friend, place a high value on what you are gaining and not what you are losing. You will waste time and energy if you do not recognize your future for the importance, worth, or usefulness it will serve you. Yeah, it may hurt, it may not feel like it is going to pay off, or it may not even look like brighter days are ahead of you, but they are.

God has moved in your life, initiating a next—a total life-change—calling for your transformation and transition. Your next is according to the plans He has for you. It involves a process of change and motion. It is connected to the purpose He has designed for your life. It will be meaningful and powerful.

PART I TAKEAWAYS

The definition of *NEXTing*: *NEXTing* is the conscious anticipation of the plans of God unfolding in your life as you engage in the now. *NEXTing* is the effective navigation and negotiation of life transitions of change.

    You must discover *NEXTing*. Remember we live life on levels; we arrive in stages as we experience seasons. As you live through life transitions of change spiritually, mentally, emotionally, physically, socially, and financially, you are discovering that you have been unconsciously and consciously engaging in *NEXTing*. You discover that *NEXTing* is the action taken to travel the distance between where you are now and where you want to be next.

    NEXTing has a voice that calls out from your future and creates a word picture called a vision.

    NEXTing helps you gain a different perspective about blindsides or the unexpected life transitions of change.

    NEXTing involves anticipating without stressing over or fearing the unknown.

    NEXTing values your future.

    NEXTing involves change. Change in life is a natural part of life's journey; therefore, expect transitions. Don't get me wrong; some changes happen without warning, but they need not catch us unprepared. You handle transitions better when equipped for them. Expecting transition is about having a mindset and heart-set that is open to growth, change, and development.

    You must expect life transitions of change to take place because one of the constants in life is change.

    You must expect transitions. Whether positive or negative, life transitions of change cause us to leave behind the familiar and force us to adjust to new ways of living, at least temporarily.

NeXT IS NOW

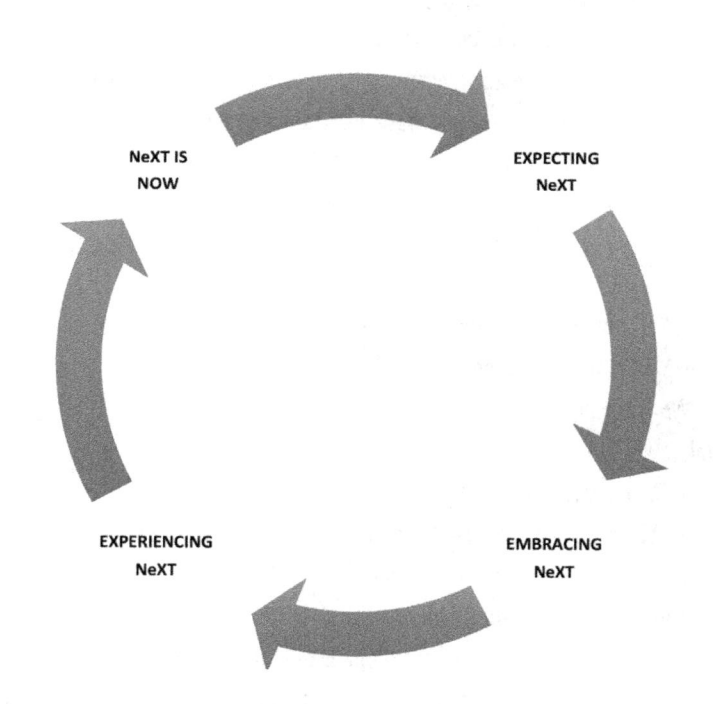

EXPECTING NeXT

EMBRACING NeXT

EXPERIENCING NeXT

PART II

EMBRACING

> *"A time to cast away stones, And a time to gather stones;*
> *A time to embrace, And a time to refrain from embracing"*
> Ecclesiastes 3:5 (NKJV)

In this section, you will learn that the wheels of transition are in motion in your life. Events have or are taking place that you need to embrace. You are discovering things about yourself and others you may not have known before. Resiliency and perseverance are character traits that produce new pathways forward for you. Embracing *NEXTing* places you at the apex of the transition and you should celebrate that you are at the halfway point!

CHAPTER 6
THE DISCIPLINE OF *NEXTING*

"Acquaint yourself with Him [agree with God and show yourself to be conformed to His will] and be at peace; by that [you shall prosper and great] good shall come to you."
Job 22:21 (AMP)

The discipline of *NEXTing* starts with a decision to embrace your next. You must decide to fully walk in the plans and purposes that God has for your life, which will require a fearless and faithful focus on your future. Right now, if you are experiencing any type of life event that is calling for a life change, it's okay, and you will be okay. As a matter of fact, you may be torn, you may be hurt, and you may be sad, but it is okay! You may be excited, you may be a little nervous or afraid, but you are going to be okay! At this stage, it is time to embrace the life transition of change. How can you truly walk in the next plan or purpose that God has for your life if you don't embrace it? Embracing transitions is accepting change. Acceptance is essential to moving on and moving forward. If you never embrace the life transition of change that you are experiencing then you will never authentically and fully move on, move forward, and move through the transition from past to present to future. When you are ready to embrace life's transitions of change, you know it's time to move. I didn't know it at the time but when and my family and I were facing our tsunami of a life transition some twenty years ago, we realized we had to embrace the transition for there to be movement toward experiencing the fullness of those various transitions. Accepting the transition initiates required movement to go from where you are to where you want to go (from now to next). The movement is an opportunity for your personal growth and development. As you decide to move forward, you are deciding and agreeing that the fullness of time has come, and you agree with God and show yourself to be conformed to His will and at peace with it. Now you are ready to do the disciplined work of *NEXTing* that leads to the prosperity and great good that shall come with your anticipated next.

The discipline of *NEXTing* involves operating with wisdom and directing your mind, thoughts, heart, and feelings toward prudence and preparation. Emotionally unhealthy and rash decision-making, combined with a lack of preparedness, will create costly mistakes in your now and next; therefore, it would behoove you to be mentally and emotionally cautious and adaptable when it comes to life transitions of change. In your eager expectation and hope, where you are looking toward your future, be determined not to self-sabotage nor frivolously act in haste, but with courage and control, decide to develop the mental and emotional discipline associated with *NEXTing*. This training is about making a daily committed decision as to what you are going to pay attention to and how you are going to think and feel so that you are prudent. It is a committed effort to keep using what you learn to maintain a healthy attitude and develop the kind of emotional intelligence that serves you well as you prepare for your next (The Key to Mental Discipline, Owen Fitzpatrick).

No matter what life transition you are facing, remember that God has designed you to become what you think, behold, and believe. Therefore, He has equipped you with the ability to think about what you are feeding your thoughts. He has designed you to consider your emotions and filter your emotions with temperance. The Laws of Exposure and Meditation are essential to mental and emotional discipline: whoever and whatever possesses your thinking, your feelings, and your will determines the course of your life. This principle must be taken seriously so that you will do everything you can to direct your mind and heart to grace.

Mental and emotional discipline is like the stewardship of the soul—just as we have a kingdom responsibility to manage the material things God gives us, so we have a kingdom responsibility to manage the immaterial things He gives us. Stewarding our thoughts, emotions, and actions is critical to effectively navigating and negotiating life's transitions of change.

Having a vision of next helps produce the mental and emotional discipline required for *NEXTing*, which helps to establish orderly movement as you navigate and negotiate the life transitions of change. It is recorded in the Bible, "Where there is no vision [no revelation of God and His word], the people are unrestrained; But happy and blessed is he who keeps the law [of God]" (Proverbs 29:18, AMP). When you wholeheartedly buy into the truth that God has thoughts and plans for you, to give you hope and a future, that will produce a vision within your heart and mind. This vision or revelation within you carries the framework of your next. This framework helps to create a mental picture that invokes passion-demanding actions that are consistent with the vision. You develop a sensitivity that is future-oriented so that you accept thoughts, emotions, and actions that are supportive of God's vision for your life. You develop a keen sense of discernment so that you can reject thoughts, emotions, and actions that are counter-productive to God's vision for your life. When you have the vision of next, you maintain mental and emotional discipline and exercise restraint, thus producing prudence and preparedness.

On the other hand, when you do not have a vision of next, you become mentally and emotionally undisciplined and cast off restraint. You are very reactionary when it comes to life transitions of change, which could prove to be very detrimental to your next. Your future is up in the air when you do not have a vision of it. Your filters are relaxed, and your guards are down when it comes to information control or the discipline of self-governance. Lacking temperate filters and strong guards, you are more likely to squander opportunities for moving on, moving forward, and moving through the life transitions of change. When your sensitivity is dull, you become open to indifference, fear, and a lack of control, which are all contrary to what is required for navigating or negotiating the life transitions of change you are dealing with.

The mental and emotional discipline of *NEXTing* keeps you operating according to principle rather than preference because you have a definite goal in mind. The mental and emotional discipline associated with *NEXTing* helps to keep your mind and heart from being all over the map and instead more consistent with what you are anticipating. In *NEXTing*, you take ownership of thoughts and emotions so that you are prudent and prepared for what is coming your way. The mental and emotional discipline associated with *NEXTing* keeps you mentally and emotionally sharp and robust, equipped for the expected and unexpected transitions of life.

NEXT Notes: "Physical training is good, but training for godliness is much better, promising benefits in this life and in the life to come" (1 Timothy 4:8, NLT).

One concern of mine when it comes to mental and emotional discipline is how easy it is to lapse into unhealthy ways of thinking and feeling when we encounter unexpected or negative life transitions. We all have unhealthy habits of thinking and feeling that we need to unlearn and discard. This is why we must give serious attention to being good stewards of all that God has given us immaterially.

The mental and emotional discipline associated with *NEXTing* subscribes to this ideology: It's all in your head and heart. Whatever problem you have with the life transition is all in your head and heart. I don't mean that the problem bears no difficult external reality. I don't mean that you're making it up or that you're faking it. What I mean is what Scripture teaches: "For as he thinks in his heart, so is he" (Proverbs 23:7, NKJV). Your thoughts become you. Your attitude defines you. Your mental and emotional habits shape you. What's going on in your head and heart governs what you do, how you live. It's all in your head and heart.

Here are a few *NEXTing* mental and emotional discipline principles that I want to share with you:

The "Switch It" Principle

Exchange your thoughts and emotions for God's thoughts and ways. God's thoughts and ways are higher than our thoughts and ways; they are different, better, beneficial, etc. It is His purposes that will prevail.

God communicates or downloads His thoughts and ways into our minds and hearts through His Word.

His Word is powerful, and He declares that His Word will not return to Him empty but will accomplish what He desires and will achieve the purpose for which He sent it.

According to Jeremiah 29:11, God has great thoughts and plans for you and your future. Let God's thoughts and ways become your thoughts and ways. Jesus told us:

nexting

> *But first and most importantly seek (aim at, strive after) His kingdom and His righteousness [His way of doing and being right—the attitude and character of God], and all these things will be given to you also.* —Matthew 6:33 (AMP)

To operate with mental and emotional discipline, you have to observe the Law of Exposure: Your mind will think most about what it is exposed to. The way that you think influences everything about you. You are what you think and feel. Jesus said that a good tree cannot produce bad fruit, like a bad tree cannot produce good fruit (Luke 6:43, author paraphrase). So, what you think about is shaping who you are and how you will respond to life transitions.

The "Think It" Principle

Tune in to the moment. Focus on God's Word or other positive reading material.

Awareness is required to help you identify with God's thoughts so that you can reject the wrong suggestions, lies, and deceptions. As you tune into what God is thinking towards you, you will begin to receive clarity so that you can take heed of what He is prompting you to think about and how you are to respond in life's transitions.

With so many things competing for your attention, awareness is required so that you can give attention to those thoughts that are most helpful, encouraging, and empowering.

What has been occupying your thoughts of late? Monitor your mind and heart!

The Law of Meditation: To do well in life, we must first think and feel well. The Law of Meditation is focused on thinking, pondering, and musing over. Pray, "God help me to see myself as You see me and to think of myself the way You think of me."

"Create It" Principle

Create a network of support. Place healthy material around you to create an environment that is conducive for your growth and development. Monitor who and what are you intentionally putting before and around your gates (eyes, ears, mouth, heart, and mind). Monitor. With whom, what, and where you are spending the most time?

The Law of Exposure: The mind will absorb and reflect whatever it gets exposed to. It is time you think about what the impact of long-term exposure is to negative and unhealthy material, events, music, movies, etc.

Create space for your mind to create other positive experiences—READ the Bible, read a book or listen to a book audibly, and have positive conversations with people. Take heed to the Law of Exposure.

The "Expect It" Principle

Maintain a flexible mindset and heart-set. Stay open to the limitless possibilities of God; your expectations will not be cut off.

A preconditioned mindset and heart-set can limit the infinite power of God in your life. Don't limit Him; it is better to remain open to godly outcomes. Refuse to be defined by the filters of previous experiences, the pains of past hurts or failures, and the opinions of others. If you expect something to happen—if God's Word or Spirit suggests a specific outcome (LOOK FOR IT)—your expectations of that outcome play a major role in its occurrence. The expectation or suggestion alone, often unconsciously, changes your behavior and your responses to help bring into reality the outcome that God declares, and you are expecting.

"New Pathways of Thinking" Principle

New situations require new pathways. It's insane to keep thinking the same old thoughts over and over again and expect different results.

God has thoughts about every situation that we find ourselves in.

God wants you to think of new pathways of thinking, even if they seem impossible.

Not only should you think God's thoughts about the situation, but you should give heed to those thoughts knowing that you will go in the direction of your most dominant thought.

"Elevate Your Thinking" Principle

Align your thinking with higher thoughts.

God's Grace can assist you in thinking on things that are above, higher, and lofty (God-class thoughts).

Because of Grace—not your efforts or works—you have been upgraded to the God class—now you must begin to think this way.

You are a prolific thinker!

We must guard against adjusting His thoughts to the natural level of man. . . . it is futile, pointless, and purposeless and will not produce the results that you are seeking.

Much of what I have shared with you as it relates to the mental and emotional discipline associated with *NEXTing* can be shared across the same platform when it comes to the physical, social, and financial disciplines involved in *NEXTing*. Why? Because when you are *NEXTing*, it impacts all of you. Remember, *NEXTing* is the conscious anticipation of the plans of God unfolding in your life as you engage in the now. I guarantee as you are embracing the life transitions of change, you are feeling or anticipating the impact it is having or will have in multiple areas of your life. Effective navigation and negotiation of life's transitions of change will depend upon you carrying similar strategies physically, socially, and financially that were discussed earlier regarding your mental and emotional discipline.

It can prove to be very challenging to prepare for your next when your now is being compromised by an undisciplined flesh.

NEXTing is most effective when you know how to possess your body with temperance.

> *For this is the will of God, that you should be consecrated (separated and set apart for pure and holy living): that you should abstain and shrink from all sexual vice, that each one of you should know how to possess (control, manage) his own body in consecration (purity, separated from things profane) and honor, not [to be used] in the passion of lust like the heathen, who are ignorant of the true God and have no knowledge of His will.—1 Thessalonians 4:3-5 (AMPC)*

It can prove to be very challenging to prepare for your next when your now is being compromised by an undisciplined flesh. Striving for mastery in your next will be equally self-defeating if your body or physical appetites are controlling you. *NEXTing* requires that you learn to say no to your physical cravings that will sabotage your now and jeopardize your next.

The discipline of *NEXTing* demands social restraint as well. Your social environment is highly critical to your effective navigation of life's transitions. The social context that surrounds you is essential to your socialization and self-actualization in both your now and your next. The right social construct can lift and inspire you as you navigate life's transitions. On the other hand, the wrong social context can pull you down and stagnate you as you navigate and negotiate life's transitions of change. It would be best if you surrounded yourself socially with a positive, reinforcing social network that celebrates you and challenges you at the same time. It is unhealthy to be in a social context that does not recognize and encourage your strengths, as it is equally ill-advised to be around people who pretend you have no weaknesses and never challenge you to grow and improve.

The discipline of *NEXTing* demands that you are intentional about the social environment that you create, live in, and avoid. When it comes to being intentional about the social environment that you create, live in, and avoid, here are a few questions to consider: Who do you most admire and why? Who is mentoring you? Who are you mentoring? With whom do you spend the majority of your time? What do your associations say about the type of person you are? The Bible is straightforward when it speaks about the intentionality of creating godly relationships. For instance, there is this Scripture in Proverbs 18:24 (AMP), "The man of too many friends [chosen indiscriminately] will be broken in pieces and come to ruin, but there is a [true, loving] friend who [is reliable and] sticks closer than a brother." When you relax in the discipline of creating your social environment, you will experience unnecessary brokenness and ruin in the *NEXTing* process. Friend, be very intentional when it comes to creating your social environment; don't link up with those who will pollute you. Leave the corruption and compromise alone. *NEXTing* directly connects to your social environment.

The discipline of *NEXTing* keeps you on the designated route that leads to the destination designed just for you with confidence.

Finally, the discipline of *NEXTing* involves financial practices that promote your future hope and good. These principles are implied in this passage of Scripture:

> *Is there anyone here who, planning to build a new house, doesn't first sit down and figure the cost so you'll know if you can complete it? If you only get the foundation laid and then ran out of money, you're going to look pretty foolish. Everyone passing by will poke fun at you: 'He started something he couldn't finish.'"—Luke 14:28-30 (MSG)*

Developing the discipline of counting the cost, budgeting, and planning are essential to *NEXTing*. Your ability to effectively navigate life's transitions can be significantly enhanced if you learn not to squander your financial resources. Remember this proverb, "Those who love pleasure become poor; those who love wine and luxury will never be rich" (Proverbs 21:17, NLT). In other words, an improper relationship with finances and material things will lead to poverty and an empty life.

> *NEXT Notes:* Your stomach cannot be your god!

Disciplines help to ensure that your personal appetites and desires of the flesh do not replace the plans of God for your life as you navigate and negotiate life's transitions of change. Disciplines will assist you in remaining focused on the goals and vision of the future that is ahead of you. The discipline of *NEXTing* keeps you on the designated route that leads to the destination designed just for you with confidence.

> *NEXT Notes:* The discipline of *NEXTing* keeps you thinking ahead and anticipating the plans that God has for you with fearlessness, faithfulness, and focus.

Read this:

> *Be strong and of good courage, for to this people you shall divide as an inheritance the land which I swore to their fathers to give them. Only be strong and very courageous, that you may observe to do according to all the law which Moses My servant commanded you; do not turn from it to the right hand or to the left, that you may prosper wherever you go. This Book of the Law shall not depart from your mouth, but you shall meditate in it day and night, that you may observe to do according to all that is written in it. For then you will make your way prosperous, and then you will have good success.* —Joshua 1:6-8 (NKJV)

This passage of Scripture speaks directly to the qualities of a disciplined person transitioning from their now to their next—fearless, faithful, and focused. Now that you have decided to embrace transition, you need to make sure that you are in confident possession of these three qualities that demonstrate your disciplined mindset and heart-set for *NEXTing*.

NEXTing is about being and doing, and what you're doing flows out of your being.

In life, and when it is time to embrace a life transition of change, *NEXTing* does not deny the reality that fearful, dangerous, and anxious events, situations, and scenarios exist, but challenges you to answer the question, "Who are you going to be?" I want to encourage you to be intrepid as you go from what's now to what's next. *NEXTing* is about being and doing, and what you're doing flows out of your being. You can take the necessary steps to go from now to next courageously and carefully because you are bold. This does not mean that the journey of life does not come with its share of uncomfortable, chaotic, or traumatic events or days where you could choose to respond in fear. But you choose to be courageous and display courage under fire. You choose to be fearless and walk by faith and not sight. Fearlessness is not fantasy or pretending like danger is not real, but it is recognizing that fear is a choice, and we need to choose the truth that fearfulness is inconsistent with your authentic self. In *The Courage to Be*, Paul Tillich writes: "He who does not succeed in taking his anxiety courageously upon himself can succeed in avoiding the extreme situation of despair by escaping into neurosis. He still affirms himself but on a limited scale. Neurosis is the way of avoiding nonbeing by avoiding being."[4]

This is what I remember when I came face to face with my decision to embrace my life transition of change and resign from my first pastorate. The culmination of the events that were at the root of my decision took me completely by surprise. I had been living in the chaos and torment of the enemy, serving through the fire. I suddenly felt a wave of fear sweep over me, quaking deep in my body, a sense of foreboding. In a dramatic moment, I had a visceral, fear-driven experience of what we were doing to the ministry and the impact it was having on the people that I believed I had been called to serve. We're all familiar with many variations of this experience—maybe an unsettling moment when worry or anxiety crept in, or the sudden terror when a car swerves dangerously close, or maybe the gnawing fear that we have a serious illness. From the personal to the universal, we're living in an uncertain world where feelings of anxiety and fear seem more prevalent than ever.

The question is, how will we respond to these challenging moments? How will we deal with fear? This question is a familiar one to many of us. Like any obstacle, fear is a doorway. As much as we may want to recoil from it, it is an invitation to discover who we really are. Who was

---

4 Paul Tillich, *The Courage to Be* (London, England: Yale University Press, 2014), 66.

I going to be? What character and actions would I choose to display in this life-altering moment? Would I be the possessor of a fearless heart and summon the strength and courage that God commanded Joshua to have? I find it quite interesting that God commanded Joshua, "Be strong and of good courage. . . . only be strong and very courageous" (Joshua 1:6-7, NKJV). When it is your time to embrace a life transition of change, who are you going to be? May you discover courage within and may you be fearless!

Faithfulness is another positive attribute to possess as a person who has decided to embrace a life transition of change. Faithfulness is being committed. *NEXTing* requires you to be committed to the process of change as you transition through it. Why? Because there are going to be moments and days from the beginning to the end that will ask of you, "How committed are you?" As you decide to accept the life transition of change you must do so with the resolve to see it through no matter what. Being faithful is having the courage to commit. There cannot be anything lasting and genuine without commitment. Commitment is the difference between being good and being great. Are you really a faithful "Nexter"? Again, for me, it is about being first and doing second. When I decided that resigning was the best action to take and I wrote my letter of resignation, I had to ask myself, "Tim, who are you, and are you going to continue to be who you are?" You see, I was committed to being authentically me. I was committed to being the best version of myself that God had called me to be. I was and am a faithful "Nexter". And being a committed "Nexter" doesn't mean you follow through on the life transition of change because people are expecting you to or because others have done something similar. Instead, you do it because that's who you are and that's what you do! A faithful "Nexter" knows it's important to follow through to achieve goals and get to next.

God told Joshua:
> *This Book of the Law shall not depart from your mouth, but you shall meditate in it day and night, that you may observe to do according to all that is written in it. For then you will make your way prosperous, and then you will have good success.* —Joshua 1:8 (NKJV)

Never quit no matter how hard the transition gets. Why? It is what you do because it is who you are. So, are you really a faithful "Nexter"?

Also, one quality of being focused in *NEXTing* stands out. I like what psychologist Ronald J. Pekala, PhD, Executive Director of the Mid-Atlantic Education Institute in Westcheser, Pennsylvania, said when asked about firewalking.

> *Ask the average person how firewalking's done and you'll hear something about a self-hypnosis gimmick. But hypnosis has nothing to do with it, he insists. Firewalking is possible through one-point focusing. It's an alteration of attention, not an alteration of state of consciousness.*[5]

When you are *NEXTing*, you must pay attention to what you are going to give your attention to. You can easily give up and quit, go in the wrong direction, or get lost in transition if you are not focused. You can choose to focus on the pressure of the moment, your emotions about what is happening in your life at this time, or the steps in front of you that are leading to your next. God commanded Joshua, "Do not turn from it to the right hand or to the left, that you may prosper wherever you go" (Joshua 1:7, NJKV). Focusing on *NEXTing* is about being an attentive person. It is about deciding to operate with deliberate attention. When you go through life transitions of change, many things will vie for your attention, but you must be deliberately focused. Whenever you are distracted during the transition, you must

---
5 PT Staff, "Fighting Fire With Focus," *Psychology Today*, https://www.psychologytoday.com/us/articles/199301/fighting-fire-focus.

fix your focus, cut through the distractions, and stay focused on the road ahead to your next.

Finally, I appreciate the way God sums it up for Joshua during his "life transitions of change pep talk", "Have I not commanded you? Be strong and of good courage; do not be afraid, nor be dismayed, for the Lord your God *is* with you wherever you go" (Joshua 1:9, NKJV). This verse speaks to you being a fearless-faithful-focused "Nexter" as you too navigate and negotiate life's transitions of change. Nexter, concentrate on your "being" before your "doing". Remember, danger is real, but fear is a choice. Fear can be reframed as an opportunity to take positive and progressive action. Don't panic or become disheveled by life transitions of change, but center yourself, breathe, and focus on the promise that God is with you wherever you go. God is with you right now as you read this book. Think about your current reality. What does next look like for you? Do you mind if I declare again that you are the "NEXT1UP"? Hey, NEXT-1-UPPER! God is with you. Let's go! It's your time and turn to traverse the land between your now and your next.

CHAPTER 7
PROCESS THEN PROGRESS

"Make a careful exploration of who you are and the work you have been given, and then sink yourself into that. Don't be impressed with yourself. Don't compare yourself with others. Each of you must take responsibility for doing the creative best you can with your own life"
GALATIANS 6:4 (MSG)

Have you ever had your flight grounded? All ready to go, packed, luggage loaded, carry-ons secure, you've gotten out of the aisle quickly, you are in your seat with safety belt secure, and you have sat through the pre-flight presentations about what to do in case of an emergency. But a voice comes on over the P.A. system that your flight has been grounded. What the ... has this happened to you more than once? Have you ever been grounded so many times and for so long that you don't even want to fly anymore? Well, if you can relate to this scenario, I have some bad and good news to share with you. Which do you want to hear first? Let's start with the bad news. The bad news is that out of all the planes that connect our world, unite families, and open our eyes to new horizons—45,000 per day on average—1-2 percent will either be grounded or canceled. So, not every flight that is scheduled to take off will be cleared for takeoff. The good news is just because you happen to get on a flight that is grounded doesn't mean you have to stay grounded. After a thorough flight check of the aircraft, flight staff, and crew are accounted for, re-calibration for onboard navigational systems and a certified flight plan, favorable weather conditions and forecast, and proper air traffic control guidance, you will be cleared for takeoff! Wheels up!

As in flying, before you get the good news that you have been cleared for runway number one and are the next in line for takeoff, you have to properly process before you progress!

Processing before you progress is just another way of saying preparation time. Think of it this way. Embracing life transitions of change is like approaching thresholds at the various open doors of life. As you approach the threshold, you are preparing to cross into a new dimension and, perhaps, a new definition of self. Thresholds can be a long, deep reflective stare that says something has changed in a relationship or as small as a glance that tells us a relationship is beginning. Thresholds can be so quiet as to go unnoticed, or they can roar through our lives with a fierceness that leaves us shattered—an unexpected job loss, a scary and voracious pandemic, a need to shed an old life, and shape a new definition of self. A processed perspective is with each threshold, you become a markedly different person afterward. Consider that after crossing this threshold, you could be standing in a different world. An example of what I refer to as a *threshold moment* is like this: it's a busy evening and you still have fifty things to do—and you get a phone call that someone you love has suddenly died. It takes a few seconds to communicate that information, but when you put the phone down, you're already standing in a different world.

You are thrust into a different world of embracing this life transition of change as you catch your breath.

How do we reconcile the profound changes that push us into new lives, new selves, and new dimensions of experience and growth? We must process before we progress. Note that in stepping through a doorway, you may experience profound change and not just geographical change. May you have newfound courage to step out of what was and what is into what will be—walking in the newness of life. Please do the threshold work because the threshold is the "place where you move into a more critical and challenging and worthy fullness."

We cannot stand nor walk into the new without first passing judgment on the past (what was and what happened)! For instance, Jesus' death and resurrection completed that work, but we must acknowledge, accept, agree, appreciate, and appropriate the "it is finished" into our lives to stand and walk in our own newness of life. This is called the "threshold work." A threshold is the end—specifically, the boundary, the end of a runway. It is the place or point of entering or beginning. Also, it is the point at which a physiological or psychological effect is produced. Processing isn't the same as talking about it over and over with no result in mind. Processing allows you to assess the situation, accept what can be done to change it, and determine the adjustments that need to be made to grow, learn, and step forward with a new approach, strategy, mindset, and heart-set.

> *NEXT Notes:* PROCESS, THEN PROGRESS!

It is time to process, then progress—the plans that God has for you should give you hope and clear and complete confidence that the way forward from here is POSSIBLE! Therefore, when you decide to embrace the life transition of change, you must let go of every wound that has pierced you and the sin you so easily fall into. Then you will be able to run life's marathon race with passion and determination, for the path has been already marked out before you (Hebrews 12:1-2, author paraphrase). You look away from the natural realm and you focus your attention and expectation onto Jesus who birthed faith within you and who leads you forward into faith's perfection. His example is this: Because His heart was focused on the joy of knowing that you would be His, He endured the agony of the cross and conquered its humiliation, and now sits exalted at the right hand of the throne of God! You cannot move on or forward without processing what happened.

> **NEXT Notes:** When you don't process what happened, you tend to repeat dysfunctional patterns.

Before you continue your journey, navigating and negotiating the land in between where you are and where you want to go, you need to make a careful exploration of who you are and where you are and then sink yourself into that, moving forward toward your next with self-awareness. You do this through what is known in the sports industry as *"self-scouting"*.

Self-scouting helps you to explore your character, the person you are when no one is looking, your habits, and your hang-ups.

You must address what I call the *"Six F's"*. You get to engage in "A retrospective" to gain a fresh perspective by reframing your past so you can properly assess your present as you chart a course for your future. Also, please consider that embracing life transitions of change helps you appropriate *"disruptive innovation"* into your life's journey.

"*Self-scouting*" is intentional and illuminating to the soul. When you are self-scouting, you are examining and evaluating your core calling, character, competency, capacity, condition, and current social location prior to totally embracing the life transition of change. Do you know who you are called to be and what you are called to do in this season, stage, and level of your life? Who are you? Who do you want to be? Who do you want to become? What of your character? How did you behave in the past? Examine what you know no one else knows or has seen that speaks to your character as a person—internally, what was going on that impacted your outcome? How you were showing up? Self-scouting helps you to explore your character, the person you are when no one is looking, your habits, and your hang-ups. Let's get vulnerable right now. How competent are you? What about your confidence in yourself? How do you feel about your current condition and social location? Do you have the capacity to make it through this life transition of change? What will impact your outcomes the most as it relates to the core of your being? Self-scouting is a good tool to have in your toolbox whenever you prepare to make a move.

Now on to the *"Six F's"*. In assessing your *NEXTing* readiness, it is key to cover the *"Six F's,"* and no, you are not flunking out! You are properly dealing with what your response was at the beginning point of the life transition of change, or you are processing the response you will choose at the life transition of change you are facing. I want you to know that I dealt with each of these responses along with the thoughts and emotions that accompanied each when I was dealing with my life transition of change (resigning from my first pastorate). It was rough, and I had to reach way down, both within and up (God), to arrive at my final response.

Which of the *"Six F's"* will your response most closely resemble? Fright, freeze, fight, flight, forfeit, or forward? A fright response may be best stated as a reaction. In fright mode, your reaction is panic-filled and chaotic. I was there. Man, fright had entered my soul. I was scared and dismayed at the same time. What was I going to do? How was I going to show up for my faith, my family, and my vision? I knew fright could not be my final answer because God loves me and my family, and His love turns fear outdoors. What is or will be your response? Are you going to let fright mode be your final answer?

Fright, if it stays too long, gives way to freeze. Yes, fright can lead to freeze mode quickly. The freeze mode is where you are stuck due to fear, dread, or an overwhelming sense of inadequacy so you choose to do nothing. Been there and bought the T-shirt! I was feeling frozen; I thought that if I did nothing, it would go away. The life transition of change that was before me would eventually just pass me by, right? WRONG! Something within me wouldn't let me go out like that—doing nothing, being indifferent, or not caring—that wasn't me! So, I did not choose freeze mode as my response. When you are in freeze mode, inertia can remain for an extended period of time. Will freeze mode be your final answer? Do you feel stuck at the intersection of this life transition of change?

Another response could be fight. Thought about that one, too! In transparency, I almost literally got into a fight with one of the deacons of the church. I grimace and shake my head in disgust even now as I write about it, how I, as a grown man, married with a young family, was *this* close—real close to fighting another man about... what, exactly?! I don't even remember now what led me to consider this as a legitimate response. Fight mode can be likened to complaining or lashing out at others over the situation at hand. Here you are, expending precious energy complaining or looking for someone to blame because nothing positive is happening in your life or going the way that you want it to go. You are blindsided by the life transition of change, so it must be someone else's fault, right? So, go ahead and fight it out, right? No! Will fight mode be your response during your life transition?

Next is the flight mode. The flight mode is running away from the situation. This is where you avoid confrontation and refuse to face what must be faced. And yes, I did consider this response several times. I thought about packing up my family and leaving this church and the ministry forever. At one time or another, this response was very attractive. As the frequency of church meetings increased during my nine months of processing before progressing, and emotions got heated, the flight mode response became the easiest option. But what of my reputation? What about my legacy? Finally, what had I done that running away would fix? Therefore, the flight mode response was not going to solve the problem. You are reading this book and considering your responses to the life transition of change that you are facing. What will you do? Will you choose the flight mode response and go off into the sunset, never to be seen or heard from again? Is this really the best option for you according to the plans of God for your life? I hope not!

Next is the forfeit mode. Forfeit mode is where you give up! You don't even show up; you simply walk away in defeat and don't even try to deal with the life transition of change. Although I thought about it once or twice during that time in my life, forfeiting was immediately dismissed as a viable option. I knew I could not give up because that would mean that everything I believed wasn't real—my God, my faith, my calling, and my vision. All not real? Impossible! Therefore, this thought came and went rather quickly. You can't stop a bird from flying over your head, but you can stop them from building a nest in your head. Now, don't beat yourself up if you have had this feeling before or if you are feeling that way right now. But I want to encourage you not to choose the forfeit mode as your response.

Finally, there is the forward mode option. This is the response that I chose, hence part of the reason why I am writing this book and sharing my experiences throughout my thirty-two years of pastoral and business leadership. As you are preparing to embrace the life transition of change that is before you, I pray that you choose this mode as your response. Forward mode is embedded in *NEXTing*. The forward mode looks all around, considers all the options, obstacles, and opposition, and concludes that the only reasonable response for a person of faith in a God who has plans for them to give them a future and hope is to march forward! After processing what had happened and what my options, obstacles, and opposition were, I concluded that my response would be to go forward. So, I set my heart and mind on forward mode. I was reminded of this verse in the Bible when Moses was leading the children of Israel out of Egypt, and when they came to the Red Sea, Pharaoh, and his army, were pursuing them. "The Lord said to Moses, 'Why do you cry to Me? Tell the people of Israel to go forward!'" (Exodus 14:15, AMPC) If you are going to get to your next, you are going to have to move forward. If you are going to cross the threshold of the doorway to a new beginning, you must go forward. And because you have decided to embrace the life transition of change that is before you, you must be willing to move forward! These are the *"six F"* options that you have when facing a life transition of change. It is my prayer and hope that you choose the last one, forward mode—march forward!

"A Retrospective" is valuable at this stage of your process of *NEXTing* because it will allow you to gain a fresh perspective before you progress by reframing your past. Gather your facts and information, close your eyes, and reflect on where you have been and what happened. Consider how you can close out this season of your life with a refreshed look at your present and what creative improvements you can make for your future. You want to go into your retrospective with liberating structures for maximum innovation. Your thought processes and probing questions should not be based on limiting beliefs and constructs of your past. You must envision yourself unboxed. As you find closure to your past, prayerfully and thoughtfully inviting selected others to share in your retrospective is an ideal way to get a well-rounded perspective. By taking

an extensive look at all your past wins, losses, and lessons, you and your personal support cohort are sure to come away with a clear idea of how to succeed in the near future. A retrospective gives you the chance to reflect on everything that happened in the most recent past and beyond, depending on how far you want to go back. Typically, a retrospective, which is a dedicated space and time for honest review at the end of a season or chapter, allows you to review a year or more in full. A thorough retrospective review transforms an expiring season or closing chapter of life into a structured approach to analyze and offer insights from the past and discuss expectations for your future (your next).

The most successful retrospectives highlight the most impactful improvements and the best ways to address them as soon as possible.

When preparing to facilitate a retrospective, consider questions such as:

What did I or we do best?

What went wrong?

How will I or we excel in the future?

What's the best path forward?

Though many approach a retrospective by highlighting what went wrong, consider reframing this period with a focus on innovating towards a more engaging and positive future. Identify the most advantageous opportunities to improve your life's effectiveness going forward according to what you believe to be the plans of God for your life. The most successful retrospectives highlight the most impactful improvements and the best ways to address them as soon as possible. Overall, a successful retrospective encourages you to improve your processes and practices to plan for a more enjoyable, engaging, and effective future. With the most appropriate framework in mind, you'll be able to design a retrospective that gets the most out of your time and those you have invited to participate in this deeper and private area of your life.

"*Disruptive Innovation*" is also a good processing tool to use before progressing. As you prepare to move forward to navigate and negotiate the land in between, you have an opportunity to become a disruptive innovator. Because the life transition of change has created a break or shift in your "normal", you can become innovative and creative in what you do going forward. As a disruptive innovator, you plan a way forward that makes your life simpler, more efficient, and even better than what it was before the life transition of change. In Luke 16, Jesus is recorded as saying that He would like believers to become creative when it comes to life transitions of change. The story describes a crooked manager who was going to lose his job because he mismanaged the affairs of the owner. Jesus says:

> *I want you to be smart in the same way—but for what is right—using every adversity to stimulate you to creative survival, to concentrate your attention on the bare essentials, so you'll live, really live, and not complacently just get by on good behavior.—v.8-9, (MSG)*

Try thinking about this as you prepare to embark on this forward journey. Are you a disruptive innovator? Do you want to be?

Embracing life's transitions of change in *NEXTing* includes taking responsibility for doing the creative best you can with your life, moment by moment (Galatians 6:4, author paraphrase). Friend, take the risk, and seize the opportunity that is before you. Allow creativity to flow through you in this season of embracing transition and transformation. What if, and why not? Be intentional about processing before progressing because you can be headed in the right direction with the wrong mindset and heart-set, thus never fully embracing the profundity of the life transitions of change you will experience along the way.

For example, in one of several instances, I recall how the principle of *"Process Then Progress"* saved me much heartache and headache. For example, one, day, we were called into a church meeting to vote on changing the church's constitution to favor the established structure and support the trustees' overreach into pastoral and doctrinal affairs. I was headed into the meeting, caught up in my emotions, and I was going to inform them that we did not need to vote, and as pastor, I consented to the change. This would have been a big mistake that I would have to pay for as long as I remained the pastor and would eventually impact those who followed me as pastor. By the saving grace of God, I processed then progressed by going through the *"Six F's"*, and discovered and decided that fright and forfeiting were not my only and best options. I chose to respond by moving forward. So, in all-out forward mode, I responded by teaching and praying with the congregation and the mob that had hidden among the congregation what God's Word says about the traditions of men and how a little yeast can leaven the whole loaf.

And in vain they worship Me, Teaching as doctrines the commandments of men. For laying aside the commandment of God, you hold the tradition of men—the washing of pitchers and cups, and many other such things you do.—Mark 7:7-8 (NKJV).

Why can't you understand that I'm not talking about bread? So again I say, Beware of the yeast of the Pharisees and Sadducees. Then at last they understood that he wasn't speaking about the yeast in bread, but about the deceptive teaching of the Pharisees and Sadducees.—Matthew 16:11-12 (NLT)

And then, we had the church's parliamentarian call for the vote. And guess what? I don't recall if we ever got around to voting that day! But I do want to exhort you to PROCESS, PROCESS, PROCESS then PROGRESS!

CHAPTER 8
THE IN-BETWEEN

"Growth is painful. Change is painful. But nothing is as painful as staying stuck somewhere you don't belong."

Embracing the different transitions in life in *NEXTing* requires you to navigate between your now and your next. Remember, as you track across this terrain, God's plans for you have not changed; even if what you are transitioning through is difficult, His plans for you are not harmful, but they are full of hope and are to prosper you and give you a future. The in-between is a time of careful exploration of who you are and your God-given purpose so that you may engage in the process of *NEXTing,* taking responsibility for being and doing your creative best with your own life. Discover who you are and the creative work that God has given you. There is an assignment on the earth with your name on it. There is a need and a solution that you have been created to meet and provide. Make a deep connection with your authentic self. After receiving the revelation, decide and commit yourself to the transition, trusting that it could be the chosen life event to help you go from your now to your next.

Let's explore navigating and negotiating life transitions of the expected and unexpected together. Right now, you are *NEXTing*, and *NEXTing* assists you in avoiding stasis and stagnation. When you are experiencing stasis or stagnation, you are not undergoing transformation and transition. When the expected or unexpected happens, you must learn to embrace both. Make sure that you don't get so absorbed and exhausted in taking care of all your day-by-day obligations that you lose track of the time and doze off, oblivious to God. The night is about over; dawn is about to break. Get up and awake to what God is doing! God is putting the finishing touches on the salvation work He began when we first believed. We can't afford to waste a minute; we must not squander these precious daylight hours in frivolity and indulgence, in sleeping around and dissipation, in bickering and grabbing everything in sight. Get out of bed and get dressed! Don't loiter or linger, waiting until the very last minute. Dress yourselves in courage and be up and about!

You see, the unexpected does not define you, but how you respond may.

One of my four grandsons, Karson, has a saying he used to say when he was younger that I love, "It's going down!" When he says this, he is referring to the moment at hand and how whatever game or activity that we are partaking in at the moment is "for real, right here, right now!" You can't ignore it or run from it if you want to get to your next, though what is happening may be harmful, not what you wanted, or what you expected. It does not excuse you from dealing with it. You see, the unexpected does not define you, but how you respond may.

Your response will, in many ways, determine your results. When you are at the crossroads of an unexpected transition, your response speaks to your character and can and will impact your next. I can remember several times, back on courtside, how I was all ready and set to get in the game because I was next. But something unexpected happened. Sometimes I did not get picked for the next game. And other times, I had to leave before the current game was over. Any way you look at it, I had to deal with the disappointing and unexpected outcome. Friend, I can remember a few times that I handled the unexpected disappointment poorly. For example, one time, because it was my basketball that they were playing with, I took it from them when I didn't get picked. On another occasion, I took my ball and pouted and demonstrated poor sportsmanship all the way home because I had to leave unexpectedly.

What I did not realize back then was that how I responded on each occasion would impact me in the future. The next time I went to the court to play basketball, the guys remembered how I reacted previously, and I was labeled as a sore loser. I had to endure this label until I changed my attitude and learned to embrace the unexpected. *NEXTing* teaches you to govern your response with the understanding that what you are experiencing is temporal. God has a plan for you, and He is going to finish what He started. God knows us far better than we know ourselves, knows our pregnant condition, and has the power to influence us, keeping us present in times of transition. That's why we can be so sure that every detail of our lives in God's grace works toward something for His glory and our good.

The losses, letdowns, and devastations we have experienced in life are not the end of the story. Our extreme trials and deepest sufferings are but the footnotes of God's greater faithfulness written into this current chapter of our lives. As Moses lifted up the serpent and delivered the people, so I say to you "Look and live." What are you looking at? What is prompting your ongoing emotional state and outlook on your future (your next)? Now is not the time to gaze into the prospects of tomorrow's circumstance or situation with an abysmal outlook. Look to God.

> *Keep your eyes on Jesus, who both began and finished this race we're in. Study how He did it. Because He never lost sight of where He was headed—that exhilarating finish in and with God—He could put up with anything along the way: Cross, shame, whatever. And now He's there, in the place of honor, right alongside God. When you find yourselves flagging in your faith, go over that story again, item by item, that long litany of hostility He plowed through. That will shoot adrenaline into your souls.—Hebrews 12:2-3 (MSG)*

The stroke and the blow in life that menaces you now fell upon Him 2,000 years ago. He took your pain and loss so that you might receive life and life more abundantly; that is what *NEXTing* in the Kingdom is all about. Change your expectations this day. The promises of God over you triumph and supersede every fear you are facing. There is no need for you to come up with some scheme or convoluted process by which things might or might not get better. It is in vain to look outward for some person to step in and answer your needs. Troubled is the one who trusts in man and makes the arm of flesh his strength. God is your deliverance. He is your Help. I am channeling resources to you even now that will reconfigure what tomorrow (next) looks like and give you a hope and an expected end (see Jeremiah 29:11). Cease pining for some instant fix or spontaneous transformation that requires no engagement on your part. God's Kingdom doesn't come through mere observation (see Luke 17:19-21), the Kingdom is present because of the personal presence of Jesus and our belief in the completed works of Jesus. Things are the way they are because of what you are doing; if you want something different, YOU must DO something DIFFERENT.

The enemy wants you to see yourself as helpless, but you are not! Nor are you powerless! It is time to break out. It is time to take up what little strength you have, what few resources are at your disposal, and move past the enemy's ramparts and towards your next. God is with you. He will bring you through. When the smoke clears, you will be left standing as you listen to His voice, act boldly, and trust deeply in His sovereign involvement in your situation. In the name of Jesus, NEXT IS NOW, and you are walking in victory! It is so!

Embracing the disheartening unexpected with the right attitude is how you navigate and negotiate this moment in your life for your next. *NEXTing* prepares you to handle life's unexpected transitions. Your embracing of what is happening at this moment in your life transition of change does not mean that you are doomed and will never recover. You are not consigned to the harmful intents or devastating outcomes of that life transition of change. By no means do you become stigmatized and stagnant. On the other hand, *NEXTing* prepares you to handle the expected transitions. You intentionally step forward with confidence that at this moment in your life, transition is what you were made for! You are in the perfect transition from a not-so-good present to an awesome future. You are released to become arrogant and cocky as if you made this happen all by yourself. You should always be humble and never forget where you have come from. You are of the *NEXTing* mindset and heart-set that God is the God of the hills and valleys.[6] The hills can be likened to the incredible, expected plans of God that are unfolding in your life. Please remember when you are standing on your hills, you didn't get there on your own. The valleys can be likened to the contrary—humbling, unexpected transitions. In the valley, you must lift your eyes to the One who sees you there. The *NEXTing* approach

---

[6] Tauren Wells, vocalist, "Hills and Valleys," Chuck Butler, Jonathan Lindley Smith, and Tauren Wells, songwriters, Jan. 20, 2017, track 4 on *Hills and Valleys*, Sony/ATV Music Publishing LLC, Essential Music Publishing.

assures you that when you are in the valley of the unexpected, you are not alone. And when you are on the mountaintop of the expected, you are not alone.

> **NEXT Notes:** God is the God of the hills and valleys; you are not alone!

This principle is on point because I recall during my trek across my in-between, I had some hills and valleys moments that needed to hear the voice of my next speaking to me! When you are *NEXTing* and you find yourself in either place, mountaintop or valley, you can be caught up or overtaken. When you are standing on the mountaintop you can become absorbed in the euphoria of the mountaintop. When you are on your knees in the valley, you can be swallowed up in the melancholy of the valley. Friend, when you're on the mountaintops of life, learn to bow low and when you're in the valleys of life, learn to stand tall. This is a perfect picture for the believer in the land in between because I don't know about you, but a lot of times, when we get to the mountaintops of life, the great experiences of life, the successes of life, we can start to think, *man, this was me, I did this, I worked this, I climbed this mountain,* but it's really in those moments that we have to learn to bow low in high places, remembering that God set us there. And you know, on the flip side, sometimes when I'm in the valleys of life, I ask, "God where are you? You left me here by myself," and that's not true either, because God sees us in the valleys, and we're not alone. At this moment of your journey, navigating and negotiating life's transitions of change, you must understand how you deal with the tension of these mountaintop and valley moments. Also, remember this: no matter where you're at, you're standing in God's grace and no matter what you have, His grace is enough! He's the God of the hills and the God of the valleys!

The *NEXTing* mindset and heart-set requires always being open for growth, development, and change even when what you are going through is unforeseen adversity or expected good times.

Friend, when you're on the mountaintops of life, learn to bow low and when you're in the valleys of life, learn to stand tall.

When you learn to embrace the unexpected transitions of life that are negative, you regain the momentum that was slowed down momentarily by the blindside. Whenever you get blindsided, you take a hit that can stop you dead in your tracks and throw you spiraling out of control if you are not prepared. *NEXTing* prepares you to absorb the blow of the life transition of change that blindsided you and use the emotional energy, the knowledge gained, and your mental toughness to live through the transition effectively by changing the unfinished narrative or rewriting the outcome. The mental toughness that you have is a result of the *NEXTing* mindset and heart-set you possess that is always open for growth, development, and change. You don't deny that what is happening is real, but it is not the end of the story. Your response helps you to control the narrative. Whatever happened or is happening does not define you, nor does it get to decide who you are going to be (your character).

For example, when you are dealing with the sudden life transition of going from employed to unemployed due to company fiscal management, you're blindsided. So, what are you going to do? How are you going to navigate or negotiate this transition? In *NEXTing*, you embrace and absorb this blow and carefully choose your response so that you control the narrative and outcome. You get to process then

NEXTing

progress by performing some *self-scouting*, working through the *Six F's* or having a *Retrospective* so you become a *Nexter* who chooses to be a *disruptive innovator*.

When you change the way you see things, what you see changes.

Your socioeconomic status may have to change temporarily, but who you are doesn't. You are still honest, talented, skillful, faithful, and employable. You are who you were before the unexpected blindsided you. While you are going through the transition, your character remains constant. And, when you come through this transition, you will be the same person unless you choose to use the transition as a part of your growth, development, and change of character for the good or the better. See, you can step across the threshold of this life transition of change as a different version of yourself and stand in a different world. Before, you were an employee with potential, and now, you are an enterprising entrepreneur starting your business in the same industry or a newly discovered one that is connected more to your purpose and passion. Therefore, in *NEXTing*, you embrace (accept, acknowledge, absorb, adjust) transition, and keep it moving forward.

> **NEXT Notes:** When you change the way you see things, what you see changes.

YOUR RESOLVE FOR NEXT

Natasha Dern says, "Determination aligns your attention and energy towards your focus." No matter what your next goals are, what you're aiming for, or what your dreams may be, one of the essential ingredients to *NEXTing* is a consistent resolve. Not only will possessing resolve help you to stay focused, but it will also help you remain calm and motivated in even the toughest of situations. In this chapter, we will explore a few areas that I hope will strengthen your resolve by aligning your attention and energy toward your next:

Pursuing the Future Vs. Being Indebted to Your Past

To fully experience your next, you must have an uncompromising resolve for it. The struggle between the pursuit of your future vs. being indebted to your past can become a roadblock, thus limiting the expectation of reaching your destiny because of the haunting horror of your past. Closure and forgiveness are powerful tools and experiences that help when you are *NEXTing* because they promote good spiritual, emotional, and mental health, which is always good for a Nexter. Your resolve for your next is greatly enhanced when you have had the proper closure and forgiveness experiences, satisfying what Maslow would class as self-actualization on his hierarchy of needs. It is not only challenging to pursue your future, but your resolution to do so can be disingenuous with open, unforgiven issues of your past still swirling around in your head, heart, and life.

Proper closure and forgiveness will clear the waste and clutter associated with your past, freeing you to pursue your next with unstoppable resolve. Without doing this, you can be stuck in between or functioning in a state of ambiguity, unable to fully experience your future.

> *NEXT Notes:* Closure and forgiveness experiences need to be designed and done well, not left in limbo.

Through closure and forgiveness, you can be delivered from the plague of your past so that you may pursue your future with passion balanced with humility. Don't let issues of your past become a plague that is stronger than the pursuit of your future! Don't let the hold of your history be stronger than the draw and pull of your destiny! *NEXTing* promotes taking the time and being intentional about addressing them through the experiences of closure and forgiveness and their accompanying tools.

> **NEXT Notes:** Don't let the hold of your history be stronger than the pull of your destiny!

What happens next? Your resolve for your next is fortified and becomes a formidable force that will propel you forward! Transformation is taking place in your life, and nothing will be the same after your next!

> **NEXT Notes:** Please note that you cannot move on to the next until you have taken care of the past and been faithful in your present. Next is waiting on those who have taken care of business.

GOD planned and purposed your life from the past to the future to be free to live in the Kingdom internally and externally for all eternity. Your freedom is not an accident, nor is it a fluke. Today, if you have accepted Jesus Christ as your Savior, you are free, as planned and purposed by God. Your freedom in Christ is the result of the planned and purposed deliverance and the redemptive power of a loving God. God did not just set you free, but He broke the power of Satan to control you ever again.

Receive the forgiveness of your sins. You are forgiven of your trespasses, forgiven of your past, forgiven of your thoughts, words, and deeds that were outside of the will of God. Forgiven—all gone!

WOW! Almost too good to be true, but you can believe the Word of God because it is the TRUTH! You are redeemed and forgiven through the blood of Jesus (see Ephesians 1:3-14)! Glory to God! Hallelujah! It is so!

Maturation

A good place to start growing up is in the land in between. Maturation is when you stop making excuses and start making changes. Your maturation strengthens your resolve for your next. When you are a person of a certain stage—not age—you are a maturing person. A mark of maturation is accepting responsibility for your thoughts, words, and actions. You were a child, you thought like a child, and you acted like a child, but when you became mature, you put away childish ways (see 1 Corinthians 13:11). Because you are a person of a certain stage—not age—you are operating with a different perspective on life.

You have a more in-depth and different understanding of the circumstances, the times, and the age in which you are living. You are desiring to operate within the plans and purposes of God; you are prepared for next—your participation in the progressive plans of God for your life. And you are *NEXTing*—anticipating and effectively navigating and negotiating life transitions of change.

When *NEXTing*, you know what to do and what needs to be done in the context of the current circumstances because you have a true north. The true north provides wisdom and understanding, counsel and might, knowledge, and an active awareness that helps you not to judge by what you see with your eyes or decide by what you hear with your ears based on worldly thoughts or emotions, but with maturity, you make decisions.

nexting

Dealing with Distractions, Disturbances, and Disruptions

These "*Three D's*" are no match for your resolve for next. The approach of *NEXTing* warns you to expect attempted distractions, disturbances, and disruptions to prevent you from experiencing your next.

Distractions. *NEXTing* helps you to stay focused on what is essential. Distractions are out-of-focus attention grabbers and energy diverters. Your energy goes in the direction of your attention. What you give attention to demands your energy. Therefore, you must remember that the attempted distraction wants your power as much as it wants your attention. *NEXTing* helps you preserve your attention and energy by focusing on what is consistent with or connected to your next.

Disturbances. *NEXTing* prepares you to expect the unexpected. Don't be moved by any negative blindsides because you expect them to test your resolve to press and progress to your next. Always see the attempted disturbances as temporal. They are fleeting attempts to annoy you, but you are spiritually, emotionally, and mentally healthy. You have a sense of peace and quiet confidence that provides you with an internal do-not-disturb mode that you control.

Disruptions. *NEXTing* helps you maintain the continuity of your progress toward your next. Disruptions seek to separate you or disconnect you from the plans that God has for you. *NEXTing* is disruption-proof because of the plans and purposes for your next comes from God, who has promised to provide for you daily. Even when we are unfaithful, He remains faithful. When the flow is from within or internal rather than outward or external, there can be no disruption because its flow is not dependent on any external source. Jesus told the woman at the well in John 4 that the water that He provides would be like wells of living water flowing out of her very own belly. But those that drank from the external physical well would be thirsty again.

Despite the attempted distractions, disturbances, and disruptions, you must be determined not to turn back and quit progressing towards your next.

Agreement Releases Acceleration. "Roll your works upon the Lord [commit and trust them wholly to Him; He will cause your thoughts to become agreeable to His will, and] so shall your plans be established and succeed" (Proverbs 16:1-3, AMPC). This passage of Scripture is asking that you take a posture that will cause your next to be established and succeed. When you come into agreement with God's plans and purposes for your life, you create the acceleration and the actualization of those plans and purposes. Agreeing with God for your life releases the acceleration and actualization because you have stepped into the eternal and timeless purposes of God for your next. The posture of agreement with God's plans and purposes is like giving God your consent to activate His plans and purposes. The attitude of agreement means that you agree to live in concord without contention, to come to one mind, and to be consistent with God's viewpoint for your next. This spiritual, emotional, and mental agreement will cause faster or more significant activity, development, progress, or advancement.

WHAT DOES IT TAKE TO EFFECTIVELY NAVIGATE AND NEGOTIATE THE IN-BETWEEN?

Let me begin by sharing this story about a Chinese magistrate who needed to select an assistant. Three men were qualified for the job, and he invited them to spend the weekend at his home. The first was a dignified older gentleman who had been a civil servant for many years. The second was middle-aged and the son of a highly placed official who had also distinguished himself as a great soldier. The third was a young man, unremarkable in every way. The story goes that the magistrate welcomed the three men into his home, and, as the weekend progressed, he observed each of them. He noticed that the older gentleman had poor table manners. The soldier was unkind to the servants. And the younger man tended to speak before listening. He was still at an impasse. The last night the men were there, he slipped into their rooms under the cover of night as they slept. He saw that the older gentleman had hung his clothes on a chair, his jacket casually tossed on the end of the bed, and his shoes were left where he had removed them. He saw that the soldier's clothes were neatly folded, but that he had left some of his personal toiletries sitting out. When he looked at the young man's space, he saw his clothes neatly folded, his shoes tucked under the chair by his bed and pointed toward the door, and all of his other belongings neatly stowed and in order. He knew the right decision to make! In *NEXTing*, you must remain clear about all things, at all times. Clarity is a reflection of the environment with which we surround ourselves. The austerity associated with many of the Eastern spiritual practices is not about self-denial—it's about discipline. And this is not the discipline of punishment, but the discipline of focus—mindful attention and expansive awareness earnestly practiced, lest you drift.

The answer to the question, "What does it take to navigate and negotiate the in-between of your now and your next?" is the discipline of focus. I believe that in *NEXTing*, it is imperative we learn to avoid living in a state of relatively perpetual emotional disarray, mental drift, or getting distracted by the eventualities of emotions, worldly thoughts, and markers of events that come up in our lives. Rather, we need to stay focused on and mindful of God's intentions for our lives and remain proactive in relationship with them. The Bible says it this way, "Awake, you who sleep, arise from the dead, and Christ will give you light. See then that you walk circumspectly, not as fools but as wise, redeeming the time, because the days are evil" (Ephesians 5:14-16, NKJV). Are you focused? Are you present and attentive to the moment? Are you tuned in to the heavenly frequency so that you may receive the transmission of wise counsel and instruction?

Cousin to focus is discernment. We are living in a time in which awareness is critical—insight based on biblical standards and discernment that will show us the narrow way between excess and stinginess, license and legalism, and innovation and sterility. In the face of a culture bombarding us with their brand of religion, it appears that the Christian faith once delivered to the saints has taken a back seat to political parties or has become identified with political parties. We are bombarded with the pop wisdom of western dualism and capitalist privilege, and the difference between true and false, real and fake, is irrelevant and outdated. Truth doesn't matter anymore. It's the fifty shades of truth that is the tone and tenor of today. It is like what Isaiah said in Isaiah 59:14 (NKJV), "Justice is turned back, And righteousness stands afar off; For the truth is fallen in the street, And equity cannot enter." Or in another instance, Isaiah describes our times this way in Isaiah 5:20 (author paraphrase): "They say that what is right is wrong and what is wrong is right; that black is white, and white is black; bitter is sweet and sweet is bitter."

We need very much to appropriate and operate at a different dimension of focus, discernment, and consciousness today to navigate the in-between!

No problem can be solved on the same level of consciousness that created it.

As you know, "No problem can be solved from the same level of consciousness that created it." When navigating the in-between, you must remember that your next will be different than where you have been. The level of consciousness needed to navigate the in-between must be of a different dimension. The biblical Christian worldview does not accept the ideology that it is the politician, the police officer, the everyday citizen, republican, democrat, independent, or libertarian that shapes society; instead, it is much deeper than that. What shapes our society are the spiritual, moral, social, and cultural influencers inside the souls of men that shape our culture.

Or to put it another way, "The environment we create is but a reflection of our state of mind. The external you see comes from the internal you don't see." At this point in the book, please take a moment and consider your spiritual, emotional, and mental environment. It has to be healthy to traverse the terrain between your now and your next effectively.

> **NEXT Notes:** No problem can be solved on the same level of consciousness that created it.

I ask this rhetorical and powerful question to many of my clients in my Transformational Coaching and Consulting business, "What's in your back seat?" The environment with which we surround ourselves is very often a direct expression of where we are spiritually, emotionally, and mentally—our global state of mind. If we are distracted, we tend to lose things. If we are disorganized, the piles begin to collect. If we are feeling disconnected, the emails pile up, and the voicemails remain unreturned. If you are starting to unravel, the first place that it is likely to show up is in the back seat. The point here is not personal cleanliness. It's about going deeper than the surface—not remaining superficial in our focus, analysis, and discernment—but performing root-cause analysis to get at what my wife and business partner often asks, "What's really going on?"

Why are the disciplines and principles of focus, discernment, and consciousness so critical for you in the in-between? Because the temptations to abort or quit the journey are real, subtle, and ever-increasing.

In my opinion, you have the responsibility to remain focused, conscious, and discerning between the true and false, real and fake, that you may be confident in your pursuit of next.

PERMISSION TO PURSUE

"For surely there is a latter end [a future and a reward], and your hope and expectation shall not be cut off" (Proverbs 23:18, AMPC).

"Know that [skillful and godly] wisdom is [so very good] for your life and soul; If you find wisdom, then there will be a future and a reward, And your hope and expectation will not be cut off" (Proverbs 24:14, AMP).

"David inquired of the Lord, saying, 'Shall I pursue this band [of raiders]? Will I overtake them?' And He answered him, 'Pursue, for you will certainly overtake them, and you will certainly rescue [the captives].' So, David went and ... recovered all" (1 Samuel 30:8-20, AMP).

I believe David had an unction in his spirit that this was not the end of the matter. Blindsided by the unexpected, it was not the news that he wanted, but he had a feeling that it was not over. David prayed and received permission to pursue what was taken from him. He was confident that what he was going through now was not final. He believed that in his next, he would recover all. And with this confidence and hope of what could be next, he pursued. And the record states that he did recover all. You have divine permission to pursue your next. And the hope and expectation of your next will not be cut off.

In the in-between, whatever your now was/is does not have to be the end of your story. Your condition does not have to be your conclusion. One time our home was foreclosed. I remember the emotional trauma and baggage this brought to our lives. But we lived through that transition, with one of our takeaways being the word "foreclosure" itself. The foreclosure was for closure. We were *NEXTing* our way through the maze of foreclosure, vacating the premises to seek temporary shelter to rent, walking through seven years of declining credit, and working to rebuild it. In the last year of the seventh year of the foreclosure listed on the report, it could not be found. (It was as if it never happened.) We now have a brand new home and homes in two different states.

> **NEXT Notes:** Your current condition is not your conclusion.

NEXTing helps you move forward with permission to pursue your next with confidence and hope of expecting something more significant or better. When you have authority in your spirit and peace in your heart, you can pursue knowing that your expectations will not be cut off. So, whenever you go through a transition, you need to understand that even if the experience is negative, it is not the end of the story.

FEET DON'T FAIL ME NOW—FAITH DON'T FAIL ME NOW!

> *Simon, Simon (Peter), listen! Satan has asked excessively that [all of] you be given up to him [out of the power and keeping of God], that he might sift [all of] you like grain, but I have prayed especially for you [Peter], that your [own] faith may not fail; and when you yourself have turned again, strengthen and establish your brethren.—Luke 22: 31-32 (AMPC)*

NEXTing teaches you that your feet of faith must not fail trekking through the in-between.

Faith functions as the foundation or feet for your *NEXTing*. Biblical faith is not "name it and claim it". Biblical faith is not luck, good fortune, or wishing. It is belief, loyalty, and trust in God with corresponding actions. Without faith, a believer cannot please God. Biblical faith believes in God, is loyal to God, and trusts in God despite what it looks like, feels like, or sounds like. Faith is so essential to the believer's life that Jesus prayed especially for Peter that his faith may not fail him during his time of testing in resisting the pressure Satan placed on him. Peter trekked from his now to his next while dealing with the adversity, the devil. Jesus told Peter that Satan wanted him out of the power and keeping of God. He attempted this by applying pressure to him, knocking him around, and beating him down. And it was permitted, but not without prayer and the assurance that if Peter would firmly keep believing that God existed and earnestly and diligently seek Him, God would reward him at his time of greatest need. In *NEXTing*, "Feet don't fail me now," should become one of your mantras when tempted and pressured to quit. Keep believing in God, remain loyal to God, maintain your trust in God, and you will be greatly rewarded. As long as your faith remains intact, it is not a matter of if, but of when!

Sometimes you must do what you have to do until you get to do what you are called to do as you navigate and negotiate the in-between.

Without the feet of faith, you will not be able to trek through the in-between—the process, the middle. *NEXTing* sustained by your feet of faith is clear. *NEXTing* is maintained by your hope and confidence that your feed will not freeze up on you. Trekking through the in-between can be arduous at times, and freezing up and quitting is a real danger. God is pulling for you! Don't let your faith fail you, keep believing—keep hope alive—keep your confidence high—you are not out of the power and keeping of God. Keep trekking through the in-between because you will make it to your next and have a testimony that will strengthen and establish others as they face their own in-between.

nexting

> **NEXT Notes:** The in-between is a good time to do a prayer life tune-up. How's your prayer life?

Prayer is essential on the ongoing journey of life, therefore pray always! Sometimes you must do what you have to do until you get to do what you are called to do as you navigate and negotiate the in-between. *NEXTing* teaches you that you are equally responsible for the in-between as you are for your now and your next. The middle or the intermediate space, place, stage, or period is critical and valuable to your success.

"In his grace, God has given us different gifts for doing certain things well" (Romans 12:6, NLT). This is the time that you put your best foot forward focusing on God's "why" (plan for you), His What (work for you), and His how (way of life for you) with as much effort and determination as possible, believing that God has given you spiritual empowerment and an endowment of grace to excel in your next. As you navigate and negotiate the in-between, meditate and confess that:

CONFESSION 1
- » You can change, adapt to change, and be an agent of change.

CONFESSION 2
- » If God permits it, then there must be a purpose in it.

CONFESSION 3
- » You are divinely authorized with God's purpose for your life.

CONFESSION 4
- » The landscape may change, but God's plans and intent not to harm you but to prosper you and give you hope and a future have not changed!

CONFESSION 5
- » You can't run away from life your whole life.

Now walk in and out what you have confessed over your life. "Death and life are in the power of the tongue, and those who love it *and* indulge it will eat its fruit *and* bear the consequences of their words" (Proverbs 18:21, AMP). You are *NEXTing*! You have decided to embrace the life transition of change in your life. Acceptance brings clarity, and clarity produces actions.

CHAPTER 9
THE WAIT (IS A WEIGHT)

"The 'Wait' is a weight that must be carried and laid aside in life."
TIM WILLIAMS

What comes next—goals, dreams, visions, desires, aspirations, things that keep us up at night, or things that set us off on our journey in life—are part of a natural order of time from when dreams become reality and our "nows" become our "nexts". This usually takes time but waiting in line is not our thing, most of the time. We live in a culture and a society that wants immediate gratification 24/7. We want our dreams to become reality overnight. We want what's next to happen right now! And we want what was planned for tomorrow to happen yesterday!

We need an elevated perspective on "waiting". I discovered the power of "the wait." The Bible says, "While the earth remains, Seedtime and harvest, Cold and heat, Winter and summer, And day and night Shall not cease" (Genesis 8:22, AMP). It is a universal principle that will never cease; it is called seedtime—and harvest, cold and heat, winter and summer, and day and night. In *NEXTing*, the effective navigating and negotiating of life transitions of change have the built-in dynamic of waiting. It is in "the wait" where you learn how to move and rest and move and rest. Rather than trying to grind it out, trying to force and make "next" happen before its timing, you learn the unforced rhythms of God's grace. "The wait" is the "and" in between the now and the next. It is the "and" between seedtime and harvest. It's the "and" between the one, two, three, and four. It's the dash between your entrance and your exit.

Because you believe that God has plans for you and plans for your future, "the wait" is where you trust God through the life transitions of change. When you are waiting, you stay focused, engaged, and active being as a Nexter. So, waiting is not being inactive or not doing anything; waiting is your walk in the unfolding plans of God. When you are waiting, you remain in conscious anticipation of the unfolding plans of God as you engage in the now. Watch this:

But those who wait for the Lord [who expect, look for, and hope in Him] Will gain new strength and renew their power; They will lift up their wings [and rise up close to God] like eagles [rising toward the sun]; They will run and not become weary, They will walk and not grow tired.—Isaiah 40:31 (AMP)

While you are waiting, you are not only keeping your expectations and hopes up, but you are also looking up, or should I say, looking forward to what is coming next. "The wait" in *NEXTing* is your time to gain new strength and be renewed in power so you can persevere to the end (your next).

"The wait" is important although we don't like to wait. We can be impatient at times. We have been conditioned to expect and to get what we want through a drive-thru, fast-food mentality. No one wants to wait; we want what we want, and we want it yesterday. So, there is tension in waiting that must be worked out.

Carry "the wait" as a necessary weight that settles you, so you don't turn the time in between your now and your next into crisis mode.

"The wait" is the weight that must be carried and laid aside throughout the *NEXTing* process. You must carry the weight of waiting by learning to be patient (exercising your power of endurance). If you don't, and you try to cut down the waiting time by rushing things, you may miss the details of the life transition of change, thus stunting your growth, development, and change. Carry "the wait" as a necessary weight that settles you so you don't turn the time in between your now and your next into crisis mode. As you carry the weight of "the wait", you are developing in character and strength. Carrying "the wait" does not lessen your "next" nor diminish you as a person. Watch this:

All around us we observe a pregnant creation. The difficult times of pain throughout the world are simply birth pangs. But it's not only around us; it's within us. The Spirit of God is arousing us within. We're also feeling the birth pangs. These sterile and barren bodies of ours are yearning for full deliverance. That is why waiting does not diminish us, any more than waiting diminishes a pregnant mother. We are enlarged in the waiting. We, of course, don't see what is enlarging us. But the longer we wait, the larger we become, and the more joyful our expectancy.—Romans 8:22-25 (MSG)

Through an elevated perspective you discover that carrying "the wait" is not a bad thing. So, carry your weight!

In *NEXTing*, you must also learn how to lay aside the weight ("the wait").

nexting

> *Let us strip off and throw aside every encumbrance (unnecessary weight) and that sin which so readily (deftly and cleverly) clings to and entangles us, and let us run with patient endurance and steady and active persistence the appointed course of the race that is set before us.—Hebrews 12:1 (AMPC).*

It is important while *NEXTing* that you learn to lay aside the weight in "the wait." The weight in "the wait" that you are laying aside are the encumbrances, distractions, and the things we readily cling to that entangle us, thus slowing down or even preventing our progress. You know what's weighing you down and holding you back; therefore, lay them aside. Ignore the distractions and get rid of the encumbrances. Tell fear and doubt to get behind you. Give anxiety and procrastination their eviction notices. Take out the bulk trash! However you want to look at it, it is time that you lay aside the weight in "the wait" so you can get on with *NEXTing* to your next. You have an appointed course of the race that has been designed specifically for you to walk or run, but you must strip off the weight in "the wait" so you can get on with it.

"The wait" is a gift that must be received and appropriated into your life before it is appreciated. "For the vision is yet for an appointed time and it hastens to the end [fulfillment]; it will not deceive *or* disappoint. Though it tarry, wait [earnestly] for it, because it will surely come; it will not be behindhand on its appointed day" (Habakkuk 2:3, AMPC). "The wait" in *NEXTing* is the game-changer! When you receive, appropriate, and master the art of waiting, you are on your way to greatness. The next that God has planned for you awaits you; it will not be behindhand on its appointed day, it won't be early, nor will it be late—it will be right on time! But you must wait earnestly for it. Don't grow weary in "the wait"!

NEXT Notes: "The wait" is worth it! Your NEXT is comin'!

CHAPTER 10
LEAN BACK (A LEANING INTO)

"For I will be leaning toward you with favor and regard for you, rendering you fruitful, multiplying you, and establishing and ratifying My covenant with you. And you shall eat the [abundant] old store of produce long kept, and clear out the old [to make room] for the new."
LEVITICUS 26:9-10 (AMPC)

Whenever there is a life transition of change occurring in your life, God is up to something for your good in His unfolding plans that He has for you. Either in God's perfect or permissive will, He will use the life transition of change to show you His regard for you and direct His favor in your life. It may not always look like it or feel like it, but the life transition of change is a God opportunity to lead you into a new dimension into your next. The life transitions of change are God's vehicle or mode of transportation to get you from one place to another. As you embrace the life transition of change, begin to see it as God recognizing you and declaring that it is time for change and for you to make a move. His leaning toward you should bring you comfort at the beginning and throughout your *NEXTing*; God thinks of you, esteems you, and cares about you. He is leaning toward you; He is turning toward you with favor and respect. Right here, right now, options and resources are flowing your way. You are attracting what you need to go to the next level. See yourself growing through this life-altering change. See yourself becoming wiser and more resourceful because God is leaning in your direction. When God leans towards you, all of God faces you, and you have God's all-encompassing presence. You get all His person, power, and purpose! And it is all good!

All you have to do is embrace the life transition of change by leaning back toward the God that is leaning toward you.

God's leaning toward you means that God is clearing a path for you, downloading the route that He has planned for you, and rerouting you, if necessary, through this life transition of change. He is equipping you with what you need to be so that you can do your best on the way to your next and in your next when you arrive. God is honoring the plans that He has for you so that you can be productive and grow and develop throughout the process of the journey. God is affirming you when He is leaning toward you by strengthening the relationship and bond between you both. It's called covenant. God is committing Himself to the promises that He has made for you. God will honor His Word and keep His promises because He is a covenant-keeping God. All you have to do is embrace the life transition of change by leaning back toward the God that is leaning toward you.

NEXT Notes: LEANING BACK means leaning into the plans and purposes of God as

LEAN BACK (A LEANING INTO) 121

God is leaning towards you. It's a NEXTing response; it's a NEXTing step.
I didn't understand this back in 1999-2000. Consider how it started. Meeting after meeting, the hostility was growing, and I was feeling pushed out by a few of the people whom I had taught the Word of God. I had believed that these few people's yeast (false teachings) had infected the whole congregation. Although seven years early, when the senior pastor had resigned to become the pastor of a much larger church in a larger city, I felt that I had gone into a bad situation and ultimately made it better, extinguishing the wrong kind of fire and eventually igniting the right one as I became their new pastor. We grew and grew and were thriving. I had grown comfortable after seven years and thought that this was going to be my first and last pastoral assignment. But eventually, that period of calm and cooperation was abruptly coming to an end. Everything that I was sure of was shifting, and life and ministry became challenging in 1999-2000.

Over a period of time, I needed to know what it felt like to have God leaning toward me with favor and regard. I thought for sure that I was no longer receiving the frontal of God but His backside. I felt as though God had turned His back on me and forsaken me. The church was growing, and the ministry and outreach were expanding beyond the four walls of the building. But I did not feel like God was rendering me fruitful and multiplying me. No, inwardly, I felt quite the opposite. Drained and frustrated. Being attacked verbally and silently. Oh, how fast things can change. Something had to give! I prayed and sought the face of God and His frontal.

In February of 2000, something broke for me and my eyes were opened. I attended a conference in Atlanta, GA at New Birth Church, under the leadership of Bishop Eddie L. Long. This conference was called *FOCUS*. It was at this conference that I met Dr. Samuel Chand. Bishop Long and Dr. Chand spoke, preached, and taught over a three-day period to over 1,000 attendees, but it felt like they were talking only to me. It was there that the Spirit of God impregnated me with the seed of Leviticus 26:9-10. I returned to Detroit on fire and pregnant! I now felt the full frontal of God in my spirit. My inner man felt God's person, presence, and power. God was leaning toward me with favor and regard. The once broken, forgotten, wounded, and beat-up pastor felt he was seen by God. God was rendering me fruitful, multiplying me, and establishing and ratifying His covenant with me despite the hell I had gone through and was getting ready to go through over the next nine months during this life transition of change!

My God, the light bulb turned on in my mind and heart, for at the entrance of His Word there is light! "The entrance *and* unfolding of Your words give light; their unfolding gives understanding (discernment and comprehension) to the simple" (Psalm 119:130, AMPC). The revelation of light that I received at the Focus Conference told me that I had to LEAN BACK!

LEANING BACK means leaning into the plans and purposes of God as God is leaning towards you; it is your response to receive and embrace what is happening in your life. I remember now that God was leaning towards me with favor and regard for me. When I started leaning back, that is when I discovered that God was leaning toward me before, during, and after the life transition of change. And He has not ceased! Friend, leaning back may look like you are giving undivided attention to the plans that God has for you. It looks like you are showing up and waiting for the strategic planning sessions that He has scheduled for you, to discuss what He is up to. When you are leaning back, you are giving God and the plans He has for you the same regard and attention He has given to you. You are showing up frontal, too! God gets your person, presence, and power. As you are embracing the life transition of change, you are present and accounted for. Life is not placed on autopilot or cruise control. You are in the cockpit awaiting the traffic controller to announce that you are cleared for takeoff... "wheels up!"

You are recognizing, welcoming, receiving, and possessing the favor that God is releasing in your life throughout the life transition of change. Leaning back means that you are open to growth, development, and change. You are utilizing the resources that God is providing for you to be productive, add value to others, and solve problems. Leaning back is receiving and appropriating the establishing and ratifying adjustments that God is making in the covenant with you. Leaning back is you actively participating in the progress that God is making in your life through the life transition of change. When you lean back, God can work through you to fully use and clear out the old to make room for the new that is coming with your next!

When you lean back, you can feel God's leaning, feel the favor, feel the love, feel the attention, feel the movement, and feel your next, for goodness' sake! You will discover that in leaning back into the grace of God at work in your life, you have the opportunity to demonstrate your gratefulness and usefulness in tangible ways. First, you can express gratitude and not walk around all entitled to the favor of God in your life. Throughout your life transition of change, God was leaning in your direction, and you don't get to walk through your transition as if you deserve His grace. At every turning point throughout the navigation and negotiation of your transition you acknowledge the leaning of God. Don't be like the nine lepers that Jesus healed and never turned to say thank you. Prompting Jesus to ask powerful questions, "Jesus said, 'Were not ten healed? Where are the nine? Can none be found to come back and give glory to God except this outsider?" (Luke 17:17, MSG) Second, your leaning back can be expressed in your usefulness, dispensing the grace that you have received throughout the life transition of change when you arrive at your next. God is taking you to another level through this transition so that you can be of greater use and make a difference in your next. Check this out:

And God is able to make all grace [every favor and earthly blessing] come in abundance to you, so that you may always [under all circumstances, regardless of the need] have complete sufficiency in everything [being completely self-sufficient in Him], and have an abundance for every good work and act of charity.—2 Corinthians 9:8 (AMP)

The leaning toward you is God making all grace (every favor and earthly blessing) come in abundance to you so that you can help others who are *NEXTing*. You can use your life transitions of change, knowledge, and experience to become a blessing to others when you arrive at your next. If you wonder why you had to go through what you have gone through, it could be so that you can share and help others. Therefore, I encourage and exhort you to LEAN BACK!

CHAPTER 11
DON'T ALLOW NEXT TO HIJACK NOW!

"Learn to appreciate what you have before time makes you appreciate what you had."[7]
ZIAD K. ABDELNOUR

WARNING! WARNING! WARNING! Proceed with caution. Don't let impatience or neglect hijack your now. Being impatient in your now will negatively impact your ability to effectively transition between your now and your next. Impatience will rob you of the process of *NEXTing* the development of the journey. Impatience with your now provokes you to rush into your next prematurely. Impatience reveals that you could be doing the right thing but at the wrong

---

7 Ziad K. Abdelnour, "Learn to appreciate what you have, before time makes you appreciate what you had," *Goodreads*, https://www.goodreads.com/quotes/899491-learn-to-appreciate-what-you-have-before-time-makes-you.

NEXTing

time. When you are impatient, your next will hijack your now and leave you with regret, and possibly, resentment.

Ingratitude for your now is a sure-fire way of allowing your now to be hijacked by your next.

Next cannot and must not be dressed-up discontent for your now! In *NEXTing*, you must be transparent and honest with yourself about your current reality. Sometimes we want to move on to the next because we are bored with our now. The boredom with our now is not our next beckoning us forward, but it could be the details that we have neglected to address in our now piling up in our minds and hearts creating restlessness that we would like to pass off as next. When we are irresponsible with our duties in our now, undone projects and unfinished chores don't magically disappear. They get reorganized in an already crowded room where, eventually, we feel life is closing in on us, and we scream "next!" so we can move on. This is not *NEXTing*; this is escapism camouflaged as progress. Ingratitude for your now is a sure-fire way of allowing your now to be hijacked by your next.

The venom of ingratitude will cause you to miss out on all that God wanted to do in your now to help you get the full benefits of your next.

> *While Jesus was on the way to Jerusalem, He was passing [along the border] between Samaria and Galilee. As He entered a village, He was met by ten lepers who stood at a distance; and they raised their voices and called out, "Jesus, Master, have mercy on us!" When He saw them, He said to them, "Go and show yourselves to the priests." And as they went, they were [miraculously] healed and made clean. One of them, when he saw that he was healed, turned back, glorifying and praising and honoring*

God with a loud voice; and he lay face downward at Jesus' feet, thanking Him [over and over]. He was a Samaritan. Then Jesus asked, "Were not ten [of you] cleansed? Where are the [other] nine? Was there no one found to return and to give thanks and praise to God, except this foreigner?" Jesus said to him, "Get up and go [on your way]. Your faith [your personal trust in Me and your confidence in God's power] has restored you to health.—Luke 17:11-19 (MSG)

Ten lepers were healed, but only one was restored to health. The other nine healed lepers were so caught up in their next that they neglected and pushed past their now, causing them to miss out on the fullness of God's plans for them. But one remembered his now; he was mindful to honor what had happened, which was his former now, and was determined not to allow the next to hijack the now. And look at the fuller benefits that he received in his next because of his gratitude and care for what was his now. This can happen for you, too, if you are grateful and appreciate the life lessons learned from the life transitions of change that you go through from now to next.

When you are discontent with your now, don't go jumping into something else and call it your next.

Whether it is an expected or unexpected life transition of change, your next must not come at the expense of your now. A hijacking is something that has been illegally seized, taken over, or taken control of. Divorce is one of life's transitions of change. However, a divorce filed by the unfaithful spouse who has committed infidelity within the marriage is a next that has hijacked the married couple's now. Marriage is another one of life's transitions of change. However, hastily getting married when you know deep down within that you are not ready for monogamy or when you are unequally yoked can both be considered forms of next hijacking now. In *NEXTing*, hijacking now for next will show itself to be very costly and disingenuous if not immediate, then over time. When you are discontent with your now, don't go jumping into something else and call it your next. Your next should organically flow from your satisfactorily completed now. When you are content with your now and have faithfully served it, you will be anticipatorily prepared for your next.

In *NEXTing*, the most common form of hijacking now is neglect. Neglect is the absence of something happening. The most common forms of neglect include:

Lack of fulfilling your responsibilities: This is the most obvious and overt form of neglect. When people refuse to fulfill their agreed-upon responsibilities because they no longer want to, this is neglect.

Emotional/psychological abandonment: When people hear the word abandonment, they usually think about being physically left behind. But that is not the only form of abandonment. Emotional abandonment occurs when people are physically present but emotionally absent. They are there and not there at the same time.

Making now a low priority: When people make what is next more important than what is now. People choose to focus on what they deem to be most important.

Not feeling heard nor seen: When people tend to look past or purposefully ignore what is currently going on in their current reality.

These various forms of neglect make it easier to hijack now with next. People are deceiving themselves when they feel they are ready for next, though they have purposely neglected their now.

For me, no matter how hard it got during my time navigating and negotiating the land between my now and my next, I was determined not to be guilty of neglecting my now. Embracing the life transition of change does not exempt you from your present responsibilities. I was not going to give the enemy nor my haters any fuel to throw on the fire or to call for a vote to remove me from my position as pastor. So, I showed up at every meeting, called or not. I preached every Sunday and taught every Bible study God graced me to do. You see, I remembered that my doing flows out of my being. Therefore, I was simply being a responsible, God-honoring pastor. My character and my calling were too important to me for me to look past the people whom God had called me to serve. I knew and believed that I had to give an account for my actions even during the tough times of the job. How can you face the people you serve every day or every week when you are just wanting to get to your next? There were some days where I wanted to make the now a low priority because I felt like they had made me and my family a low priority. But that ended up as a no-go; I couldn't do that. Instead, I kept my prayer life healthy and remembered that God was the God of the both the hills and the valleys. If you ever feel like your now is being hijacked by your next, then I encourage you to do a quiet *Retrospective* so you can reframe what you are feeling and what is happening to you or around you.

The biggest form of neglect that I wrestled with throughout the nine months of navigating and negotiating my life transition of change was emotional/psychological abandonment. The neglect that comes from emotional/psychological abandonment is odorless and colorless; it can't be readily detected. You can be present and not be present, and no one from a distance knows. You can fake it for a while and no one from a distance or in a crowd will pick up on it. It becomes evident over time with persons whom you are interacting with very closely, and it is ultimately revealed in you. Was I really there, or was I going through the motions pretending that I was there? Was I keeping people at a distance so that they would not pick up on the fact that I was emotionally abandoning them? Had I checked out, deceiving myself by serving with lifeless actions? I am not going to lie to you, I was not neglecting those people by emotional/psychological abandonment. But there were also times when I was not emotionally available for my own well-being and self-care. So, I had to be honest with myself and constantly do some *Self-scouting*. The Holy Spirit and my wife, who is my accountability partner, helped me through the spiritual warfare. I thank God for the Holy Spirit and my wife because they helped me prevent my next from hijacking my now. Through the disciplines of *NEXTing*, I was able to stay engaged and actually grow and develop, and I was transformed through the life transition of change I was going through. Today, my self-care is a priority that helps me be the best version of myself daily.

What about you? Do you feel that you are neglecting your now? Are you looking past now to get to where you want to be? Are you present but not there? Has your now become a hijacking victim of your next? You can change that right now. You do not have to continue down the path of neglect. H.A.L.T. and breathe! Process then progress! Why? Because where you are now was once your next. And eventually your next will become your now!

NEXT Notes: There is a direct correlation to how you are managing your now that impacts your capacity and ability to function in what is to be your next.

PART II TAKEAWAYS

The discipline of *NEXTing* starts with a decision to embrace life transitions of change.

Discipline is regulated action in accordance with a particular system of governance. Discipline is commonly applied to regulating human behavior. Discipline is training, leading, and bringing oneself into subjection or compliance to the will of a master. In the academic and professional worlds, a discipline is a specific branch of knowledge, learning, or practice.

The discipline of *NEXTing* involves navigation and negotiation through the distance between where you are now and where you want to be next.

Process then progress: Fright, Freeze, Fight, Flight, Forfeit, or Forward; you choose your response.

The in-between: Acceptance brings clarity, and clarity produces actions. Your acceptance is the beginning of the journey through the in-between.

The wait is a weight: You must learn how to wait so that you can carry the weight of *NEXTing*.

Leaning back is a leaning into: When you lean back, you feel the lean of God and His favor, love, regard, increase, and your next.

Avoid the hijacking of now by next: When you are discontent with your now, don't go jumping into something else and call it your next

Embracing transitions: Whether positive or negative, life transitions cause us to leave behind the familiar and force us to adjust to new ways of living, at least temporarily. Embracing transition will allow you to actively participate in your progress. When you embrace change, you are taking ownership of it and the responsibility that comes with that ownership. Your embrace of transition sends a message to the transitional moment that you are in that you are not just along for the ride, but that you are confident that you can respond appropriately throughout the life transitions of change.

NeXT IS NOW

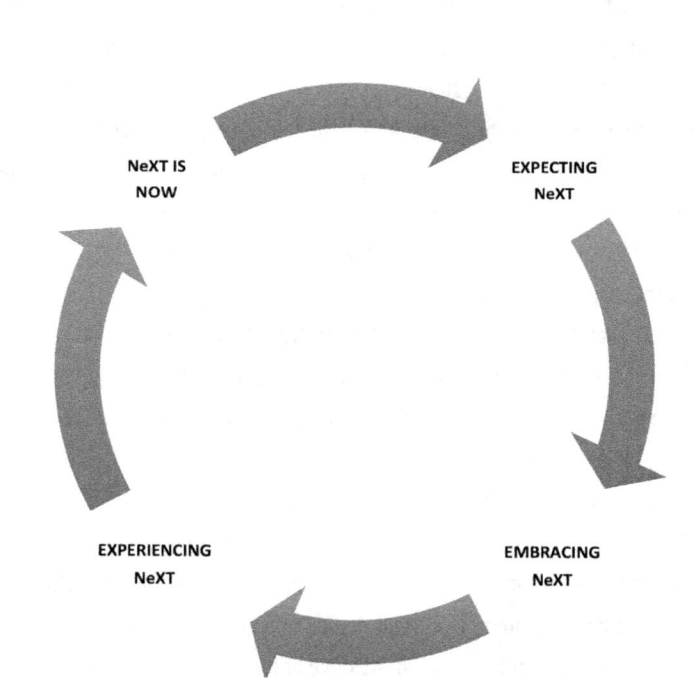

EXPECTING NeXT

EXPERIENCING NeXT

EMBRACING NeXT

PART III

EXPERIENCING

Since this is the kind of life we have chosen, the life of the Spirit, let us make sure that we do not just hold it as an idea in our heads or a sentiment in our hearts, but work out its implications in every detail of our lives.
GALATIANS 5:25 (MSG)

When you are experiencing transition, you are going from your now to your next. The plans that God has for you are unfolding before you, and by grace through faith, you are working the process. You are accepting and confirming that it is in God that you live, move, and have your being. There is a difference between existing and living, between surviving and thriving. In this section, we are going to explore how you can live through transition rather than just simply exist while transition is happening. We will discuss how you can thrive in transition and not just survive the transitions of life. In committing to experiencing life's transitions, you are deciding to live in committed actions that make the transitions work for your growth and development as a person rather than acknowledging that a transition is taking place. You will learn how to experience life's transitions effectively and efficiently because you anticipated them, acted, and strategically responded rather than reacted. It is time to celebrate that you are *NEXTing!*

CHAPTER 12
THE DYNAMICS OF *NEXTING*

"For His divine power has bestowed on us [absolutely] everything necessary for [a dynamic spiritual] life and godliness, through true and personal knowledge of Him who called us by His glory and excellence."
2 Peter 1:3 (AMP)

The definition of dynamics is a pattern or process of change, growth, or activity. *NEXTing* itself is dynamic and experienced throughout the different life transitions of change. Life is lived on levels; we arrive there in stages as we experience different seasons. Another definition of dynamics is the study of the driving forces that describe a system and how it causes change, growth, or activity.

Purpose inspires and compels you to say "yes," infusing you with the courage to say "no."

---

nexting

The dynamics of *NEXTing* can be described this way: at various life transitions of change in which we make decisions, the constant, implanted driving forces that cause change, growth, or activity are present because they are within us. The driving forces of *NEXTing* have been divinely given to us: "For His divine power has bestowed on us [absolutely] everything necessary for [a dynamic spiritual] life and godliness" (2 Peter 1:3, AMP). It is through true and personal knowledge of them and their source that we can experience the process of change, growth, and activity involved in *NEXTing*. The dynamics of *NEXTing* help us effectively navigate and negotiate life transitions of change.

Some of the dynamics of *NEXTing* are purpose, vision, passion, timing, patience, stewardship, exhortation, wisdom, decisiveness, and grace. For each dynamic, I want to give you space and time to respond to the following questions I have posed to you at the end of each. Then, I encourage you to:

THINK ABOUT IT!
PRAY ABOUT IT!
DREAM ABOUT IT!
WRITE ABOUT IT!
TALK ABOUT IT!
BE ABOUT IT!
NEXT IT!

PURPOSE

The divine sense of purpose implanted in the human heart is a dynamic of *NEXTing*. When you don't know the meaning of a thing, abuse is inevitable. Therefore, God gives you a sense of purpose so that you can effectively navigate and negotiate life transitions of change. This dynamic proves invaluable when what you are facing tests the very fabric of your being and shakes you to the core of your existence. Purpose calls you back, drives you back, calls you forward, propels you forward, or helps you stand still, avoiding the pressure of others to shift it. When a transition has disrupted your flow and caused you to drift from your assigned path or when you have veered off-course due to some interruption in life, purpose is there as your constant and true north. Purpose gets you up in the morning and keeps you engaged throughout the day. Purpose inspires and compels you to say "yes," infusing you with the courage to say "no." In the dynamics of *NEXTing*, the driving force of purpose propels you forward with an unstoppable momentum through the various transitions of life.

It was the dynamic of purpose that kept me going from the point that I became spiritually impregnated with the seed of change, growth, and activity at the Focus Conference in February, 2000. As I was experiencing *NEXTing*, purpose inspired me to push past the redundant passion-draining and dream-killing meetings that I had to endure. While I was navigating and negotiating my life transition of change, my purpose and why was what kept me through each trimester of the pregnancy to the point of delivery. The purpose dynamic of *NEXTing* helped me birth my next when the time had arrived.

On another instance I recall how a divine sense of shared purpose in our marriage helped my wife, Lisa, and I, transition to being empty nesters—after raising three children—with a grace that did not break our stride or cause a setback. This driving force aided us tremendously and helped us avoid the dreadful space of being a married couple whose child-rearing responsibilities had ended. Because of purpose, we did not find ourselves as two strangers bumping in the night or allow our marriage to deteriorate into crisis survival mode. Purpose—knowing who you are, why you are, and what you are to do—is a driving force that will have you thriving in life before, during, and after different life transitions of change.

What about you? How are you doing at this stage of your journey to your next? As you are experiencing *NEXTing*, do you see your purpose?

Who are you being and what are you doing with the purpose that you have been given at this intersection between where you are now and the life transitions of change? And finally, what role is purpose playing for you through the life transition of change you are experiencing?

VISION

In the dynamics of *NEXTing*, vision is the picture of something different and better that God has for you and shows you in your mind and heart. It is the prearranged and ordained good life that He has prescribed for you before the foundation of the world. No vision, no future. Vision is very important for *NEXTing* because it invites you to imagine and dream about what's next. Vision is future-oriented, which is good, because God wants you to look at what is in front of you rather than focusing on what is behind you. Remember, vision can assist you in putting your past in its proper place—behind you—and keeping it there. Vision will help you change, grow, and engage in *NEXTing* throughout the life transitions of change. Therefore, never stop dreaming and never stop believing in good things concerning your future.

Vision helps you look into the future and the possibilities that lie ahead. Vision is a necessary dynamic in *NEXTing* because, without it, you will return to your past or always live in your past. Some people always live in yesterday and never today or tomorrow because they have not perceived that God has given them one. They have not considered the possibilities that are in front of them despite the challenges, obstacles, or opposition that the life transition of change presents.

> ***NEXT Notes:*** Don't ever stop dreaming and imagining as long as there is breath in your body! Who knows what the tide and time may bring into your life.

This is true for an individual, a family, a community, a city, an organization, or even a nation. Vision helps you effectively navigate and negotiate life transitions of change as you move towards your next so you don't go backwards, get stuck, or reduce your living to just surviving because you are only living in what was. You were created for more and different; you were created to live and to thrive! Check out Luke 24: 13-17, 21, 25, 30-32 (AMPC).

> *And behold, that very day two of [the disciples] were going to a village called Emmaus, [which is] about seven miles from Jerusalem. And they were talking with each other about all these things that had occurred. And while they were conversing and discussing together, Jesus Himself caught up with them and was already accompanying them. But their eyes were held, so that they did not recognize Him. And He said to them, "What is this discussion that you are exchanging (throwing back and forth) between yourselves as you walk along?" And they stood still, looking sad and downcast.*
>
> *But we were hoping that it was He Who would redeem and set Israel free. Yes, and besides all this, it is now the third day since these things occurred.*
>
> *And [Jesus] said to them, "O foolish ones [sluggish in mind, dull of perception] and slow of heart to believe (adhere to and trust in and rely on) everything that the prophets have spoken!" And it occurred that as He reclined at table with them, He took [a loaf of] bread and praised [God] and gave thanks and asked a blessing, and then broke it and was giving it to them When their eyes were [instantly] opened and they [clearly] recognized Him, and He vanished (departed invisibly). And they said to one another, "Were not our hearts greatly moved and burning within us while He was talking with us on the road and as He opened and explained to us [the sense of] the Scriptures?"*

NEXTing

This portion of Scripture speaks to the importance of vision in the dynamics of *NEXTing*. Let's unpack it: The life transition of change was the death of Jesus Christ, the Messiah. These two disciples of Jesus are discussing what has happened and because they have no vision of the future, they are stagnated and stuck living in their past. They are without hope for their future! The Bible says, "their eyes were held, so that they did not recognize Him" (v.16). What was holding their eyes? Friend, we see (perceive) with our minds and hearts as we look through our eyes. Their eyes were held preventing them from recognizing Jesus because they were consumed with the past; therefore, it was their preoccupation with yesterday that prevented them from having a vision of tomorrow.

When you don't have a vision of the future, you will choose to live your life in the past.

Lean in and listen to what they were thinking and feeling when Jesus asked them what they were discussing. The Bible says, "And they stood still, looking sad and downcast . . . But we were hoping" (v. 17, 21). Standing still and looking sad and downcast is reflective of their lack of vision for the future. Note that they had hopes but they had been dashed. All of this is because they had no vision of the future. But when their eyes were opened through the understanding of the Word, vision was restored and they were moved and compelled to go forward and share with the others the good news of the possibilities that lie ahead of them and the world. Friend, I remind you that without vision, there is no future. When you don't have a vision of the future, you will choose to live your life in the past.

The dynamic of *NEXTing*'s vision is what compelled me to believe as I was navigating and negotiating my life transition of change to not be a foolish Nexter [sluggish in mind, dull of perception] and slow of heart to believe (adhere to and trust in and rely on) everything that God had planned for me.

What about you? How are you doing at this stage of your journey to your next? As you are experiencing *NEXTing*, do you see the vision of your future? Who are you being and what are you doing with the vision that you have been given at this intersection between where you are now the life transitions of change? And finally what role is vision playing for you through the life transition of change you are experiencing?

PASSION

Ambition is defined as an ardent desire to achieve a particular end. In the dynamics of *NEXTing*, ambition is the mysterious longing that nothing under the sun can satisfy except God (see Ecclesiastes 3:11). God places this mysterious longing as the driving force within your heart so that you will not become complacent and stagnant in life, or settle for an unfulfilled life when you should be moving forward to next. In the dynamics of *NEXTing*, divinely given ambition keeps you hungry for the best that God has for you. It will help you to keep it moving when you are tempted to give in, give up, or give out. When going through life transitions of change, you must have grit and determination so that your life does not become a casualty of the life event that you are dealing with. Even if the life transition of change knocks you down, the ambition associated with the dynamics of *NEXTing* exhorts you from within to arise from the depression and prostrations that circumstances have kept you and keep pressing towards your goal (see Isaiah 60:1). Nothing under the sun can satisfy the driving force of this mysterious longing except for God, and He does not afford you the leisure to believe that you have it all together or that you have made it. But, through every life event, you believe that you are well on your way because you are reaching out for that which has so mysteriously reached out for you. The mysterious longing is the driving force that helps you to keep your eyes on the goal, where God is beckoning you onward.

It's hard to keep *NEXTing* when your passion has waned. No passion, no momentum! You get up and get going when you are passionate about something. Passion helps you to endure and give your all while you are navigating and negotiating life transitions of change. It was the passion for life and ministry that propelled me through the dark nights and long days between now and next. With passion I was able to overcome the temptation to let my next hijack my now through neglect, particularly the emotional and psychological abandonment that I was often tempted to yield to. A passionless Nexter is a Nexter who doesn't go very far, if at all.

I recall one particular instance when I was experiencing my life transition of change. One of the haters showed up for Sunday service with his Detroit Freepress newspaper. As I was preaching and teaching the Word of God, he positioned himself sideways on a pew, legs. He unfolded the paper, shook it very loudly, and proceeded to read it, rudely drawing attention to himself and his ignorance. If it was not for my passion for my faith and my calling, I can only imagine how far this attack would have set me back or created a very long delay in my progress. I probably would have been arrested for assault and battery that day had I acted on the thoughts that were going through my mind at the time. It was my passion to preach in and out of season—when it was convenient and comfortable and when it was not—that fueled my fire. I had to preach when they wanted to hear and when they didn't! The Bible says,

> *Preach the word! Be ready in season and out of season. Convince, rebuke, exhort, with all longsuffering and teaching. For the time will come when they will not endure sound doctrine, but according to their own desires, because they have itching ears, they will heap up for themselves teachers; and they will turn their*

> *ears away from the truth, and be turned aside to fables. But you be watchful in all things, endure afflictions, do the work of an evangelist, fulfill your ministry.* —2 Timothy 4:2-5 (NKJV)

You can take this admonition and exhortation and apply it to whatever you have been called to be and do or what you are *NEXTing* towards. Whatever it is, you must possess the passion for it if you are going to endure and maintain momentum throughout the life transition of change you are experiencing.

What about you? How are you doing at this stage of your journey to your next? As you are experiencing *NEXTing*, how is your passion level? Who are you being and what are you doing with the passion that you have been given at this intersection of the now and your life transitions of change? Finally, what role is passion playing for you through the life transition of change you are experiencing?

> ***NEXT Notes:*** No passion, no momentum! Passion is like adding fuel to fire.

TIMING

Timing is the ability to select the precise moment for doing something for optimum effect. Throughout the Bible, the perfection of God's timing is a dominant theme. With God, things happen in the fullness of time. The fullness of time is the right time, the appropriate time, or the time that has been appointed or ordained. You may have heard the idiom, "He may not come when you want Him to, but He is always on time!" The devout Bible reader knows that there is an opportune time to do things—a right time for everything on the earth. Thus, the God who knows the plans that He has for you—plans to prosper you and not to harm you, plans to give you hope and a future—has also been perfectly timed. Deeply connected to the rhythms of your life, the consciousness of the perfect timing of God is a part of the dynamics of *NEXTing*. Life events and interruptions can cause disruption and throw your life in an out-of-control spiral. However, the timing aspect can create peace and calm, allowing you to change or grow through the transition. Believing and trusting that everything is made beautiful and appropriate in its time is an underlying cause of change or growth. A trustful awareness of the perfect timing of God will help you navigate and negotiate through some of the most challenging events of your life. In the dynamics of *NEXTing*, timing helps you to remain calm, peaceful, and patient because you are operating in a dimension where you believe that everything will be made beautiful and appropriate in its time.

For me, the timing of God was fascinating because it was like the timing of a woman who has been impregnated, conceives, and carries that seed for nine months, through trimesters to full-term birth, nine months later. My life transition of change was from February 2000 to November 2000. I did not notice at the time, but God's timing was impeccable and perfect. Timing is a very powerful dynamic. God is not limited or bound by our timetables. Do you know that God picks the time, place, and circumstances that He speaks to us? I recall the timing of God in the dynamics of *NEXTing* when I revisited God's life transition of change with Abraham concerning the birth of the promised seed or son, whom he was to name Isaac, in the book of Genesis.

Ages seventy through one hundred covers a thirty-year period of time in the life of Abraham. Abraham was seventy years old when God first appeared to him, and he was seventy-five when he finally left his home and country to go to a land that God would show him. Then, ten years go by, and God did not appear to him again to remind him of the promise for his future until he was eighty-five. Then God appeared again when Abraham was at the ripe old age of ninety-nine. God tells him he is going to have a child that will be the fulfillment of His promise to him. And then it was when Abraham was one hundred years old that the promise of his future (his next) was fulfilled in the birth of his son, Isaac. You see, it is in the timing of God that you get to your next! You are going to need to trust the dynamic timing of God as you navigate and negotiate the life transitions of change.

What about you? How are you doing at this stage of your journey to your next? As you are experiencing *NEXTing*, how is your relationship with the timing of God? Who are you being and what are you doing with the timing that you have been given at this intersection of now and transition? What role is timing playing for you through the life transition of change you are experiencing?

Take a moment to answer these questions, and, as always, THINK ABOUT IT! PRAY ABOUT IT! DREAM ABOUT IT! WRITE ABOUT IT! TALK ABOUT IT! BE ABOUT IT! NEXT IT!

PATIENCE

"For you know that when your faith is tested it stirs up in you the power of endurance. And then as your endurance grows even stronger, it will release perfection into every part of your being until there is nothing missing and nothing lacking" (James 1:3-4, TPT). Patience is the power of endurance. In the dynamics of *NEXTing*, patience is irreplaceable and invaluable. If you want to navigate and negotiate the life transition of change that you are experiencing effectively, you must be patient. You need to maintain and use your power of endurance that has been given to you. So, when you are moving towards your next, your ability to endure grows stronger, and it will release perfection into every part of your being until nothing is missing and nothing is lacking—you arrive at your next "READY!"

STEWARDSHIP

The managing of the resources that have been entrusted to you as you effectively navigate and negotiate change and continuity throughout the transitions of life. You have in your possession time, treasures, talents, and relationships that must be properly stewarded through change while maintaining continuity in your now and your next.

God is the owner of your now and your next and He has given you stewardship as a responsibility in your *NEXTing*. You are expected to manage both your now and your next as a faithful steward for change and continuity. The dynamic of the stewardship mindset and heart-set helps you have a sense of mindfulness, consciousness, sensitivity, and awareness that you will give an account. As you experience *NEXTing*, you are paying attention to the details in your now for continuity in the changes of your next. The dynamics of *NEXTing* through stewardship helps you with all the details that go unnoticed by others on the outside, and they make all the difference when you understand the importance of change and continuity in your now and your next. Stewardship gives you the base to work from and makes you ready for the unexpected and expected life transitions of change. Change is inevitable between now and next, but the continuity between the two is where the dynamic of stewardship comes into play for your effectiveness and success moving forward. Stewarding both the change and continuity helps you stay on the same wavelength as God's desires and plans for you. You cannot just do what you want to do and expect to get the results that God wants for you. The driving force of stewardship keeps you in step and on track for the journey towards your next.

What about you? How are you doing at this stage of your journey to your next? As you are experiencing *NEXTing* how is your Stewardship of your now and your next? Who are you being and what are you doing with the Stewardship that you have been given at this intersection of the life transitions of change that you find yourself? And finally what role is Stewardship playing for you through the life transition of change you are experiencing?

EXHORTATION

"David was greatly distressed, for the men spoke of stoning him because the souls of them all were bitterly grieved, each man for his sons and daughters. But David encouraged and strengthened himself in the Lord his God" (1 Samuel 30:6, AMPC). Another driving force in the dynamics of *NEXTing* is exhortation. Your next will talk to you; it will call out to you; it will encourage you; it will be a voice deep within that you hear clearly and specifically. In the dynamics of *NEXTing*, the exhortation I refer to are the words you say to yourself and the stories you are telling yourself. What are you telling yourself about your now and your next? You have been given the exhortation (self-talk) to strengthen and encourage yourself as you navigate and negotiate life transitions of change. So, what does it sound like when you listen to you? What are you telling yourself daily?

The God-inspired words you speak daily will perform wonders for your soul.

I don't about you, but I, like David, find it necessary to strengthen and encourage myself with my own words daily. I developed mantras that I would tell myself every morning and still today. Do you have a mantra to encourage yourself? Are you strengthened or do you feel like quitting once you talk to yourself? "NEXT1UP!" "IT'S MY TIME AND MY TURN!" "NEXT IS NOW!" "I GOT NEXT!" "I AM *NEXTing* MY WAY TO MY FUTURE!" "I AM A NEXTER!" These mantras keep me strengthened and encouraged. The Bible says, "David was greatly distressed, for the men spoke of stoning him." How do you go from being greatly distressed to strengthened and encouraged? I am glad you asked—by what you say to yourself! The God-inspired words you speak daily will perform wonders for your soul. Talk to yourself, my sister! Exhort yourself, my brother! Always be mindful of what you say to yourself. If you are talking negatively, stop it! If you are beating yourself up, stop it! If you are lying to yourself, stop it!

> *Let no foul or polluting language, nor evil word nor unwholesome or worthless talk [ever] come out of your mouth, but only such [speech] as is good and beneficial to the spiritual progress of yourself and others, as is fitting to the need and the occasion, that it may be a blessing and give grace (God's favor) to yourself and those who hear it.—Ephesians 4:29 (AMPC)*

What about you? How are you doing at this stage of your journey to your next? As you are experiencing *NEXTing* how is your exhortation (your self-talk)? Who are you being and what are you doing with the Exhortation that you have been given at this intersection of the life transitions of change that you find yourself? And finally what role is exhortation playing for you through the life transition of change you are experiencing?

NEXT Notes: What you say to yourself matters. The words or stories you tell yourself can be the difference between staying where you are and moving forward towards your next. Does your self-talk strengthen and encourage you?

WISDOM

God makes His driving force of wisdom readily available for the asking when you are addressing life events that demand those crucial decisions. Wisdom from above is at your disposal. God desires that His plans for you have an expected end. In other words, He is committed to you living out your ordained destiny, and He will supply you with the wisdom necessary to accomplish this. Isaiah 30:21 (NKJV) puts it this way: "Your ears shall hear a word behind you, saying 'This is the way, walk in it.' Whenever you turn to the right hand or whenever you turn to the left." God provides you with the wisdom to make the right turns at the right times.

When was the last time you asked God about your future? Where will you be in your immediate and long-term future? Who do you want to become? These are questions for you to answer and discover. Be transparent—chances are you may feel that you should be further along than you are. Or you may feel clueless about your future. If you are not careful, you will slip into a self-pity mode, thus taking yourself out before you can get started doing something about where you are and where you want to go. You do not have to live life meandering through mediocrity. In the dynamics of *NEXTing*, the driving force of wisdom assists you in co-dreaming and possibility-thinking with God so that you are aligned with His future for you. This is great news! God has given you the ability to participate in creating your destiny. Isn't it surprising how many people never accept this gift—or give it away—making someone else responsible for it?

When you allow someone other than God to be the custodian of your future, you are at a grave disadvantage in life. Your next becomes the toy or video game that others trivialize and eventually discard due to boredom. The dynamics of *NEXTing* help you take your life back and sync up with God's master plan through the driving force of wisdom.

What about you? How are you doing at this stage of your journey to your next? As you are experiencing *NEXTing* how is relationship with the timing of God? Who are you being and what are you doing with the Timing that you have been given at this intersection of the life transitions of change that you find yourself? And finally what role is timing playing for you through the life transition of change you are experiencing?

DECISIVENESS

Only it must be in faith that he asks with no wavering (no hesitating, no doubting). For the one who wavers (hesitates, doubts) is like the billowing surge out at sea that is blown hither and thither and tossed by the wind. For truly, let not such a person imagine that he will receive anything [he asks for] from the Lord, [For being as he is] a man of two minds (hesitating, dubious, irresolute), [he is] unstable and unreliable and uncertain about everything [he thinks, feels, decides].—James 1:6-8 (AMPC)

The dynamic of *NEXTing* makes the *NEXTing* experience fuller when you are decisive. Decisiveness helps you to move forward with stability and consistency towards your next from your now. When you are navigating and negotiating the life transitions of change, being decisive is to your advantage because you cannot afford to waver and doubt when you're so close to your destination. You could be one decisive turn away from the breakthrough of your next. At this stage, you have gone through too much to stop now! You cannot afford to be a man of two minds—hesitating, dubious, irresolute, unstable, unreliable, and uncertain about everything you think, feel, and decide. You are on the brink of your next; be decisive and commit to crossing over into your new beginning!

On the eve of my big announcement that I would be resigning on that first Sunday of November 2000, I knew that if I wanted to experience all that God had planned for me, I had to be decisive. Not only my future, but my family and the lives of others, would be spiritually impacted by my decision, and they would need a decisive man in that moment. I decided I wanted to be God's man, a decisive man! The winds of adversity and uncertainty did not toss me about within nor discourage me from making one of the biggest decisions of my life and ministry.

What about you? How are you doing at this stage of your journey to your next? As you are experiencing *NEXTing* how is your decisiveness? Who are you being and what are you doing with the ability to be Decisive that you have been given at this intersection of the life transitions of change that you find yourself? And finally what role is decisiveness playing for you through the life transition of change you are experiencing?

GRACE

Grace is the last driving force of the dynamics of *NEXTing* that I would like for you to consider with me. Grace is God's enablement. The driving force of grace enables you to do all the things He has called you to do, strengthening and empowering you to fulfill His purpose. This driving force makes you sufficient, ready for anything, and equal to anything through Him who infuses you with inner strength and confident peace (see Philippians 4:13). Whatever you feel is overwhelming and impossible to deal with in life, the driving force of grace will enable you to confront with an inner strength and confident peace that promotes change and growth. The driving force of grace gives you the resiliency to continue pressing forward towards your next despite the intimidating difficulties that accompany life transitions of change. You are graced to be what you need to be in the moments of transition. And you are graced to do what the moment is demanding. When appropriated in your life, grace becomes your sufficiency and efficiency as you next from your present to your future.

It was grace that welled up inside of me and allowed me to stand flatfooted and deliver my last message and then submit my letter of resignation on that Sunday morning. Through the swirling thoughts and emotions, I had assurance that I had been faithful over a few things and that God was transitioning me into my next. It was only by God's grace that I did not feel like a failure, and therefore I could return that

nexting

same Sunday afternoon and attend my last anniversary concert as the pastor with my head held high even though I felt the sadness in the air. Let no one tell you that life transitions of change are all joy and no tears. Sometimes the transitions are bittersweet, but grace enables you to endure the trade-offs.

What about you? How are you doing at this stage of your journey to your next? As you are experiencing *NEXTing* how is Grace impacting you? Who are you being and what are you doing with the Grace that you have been given at this intersection of the life transitions of change that you find yourself? And finally what role is Grace playing for you through the life transition of change you are experiencing?

NEXT Notes: The dynamics of *NEXTing* renders you poised and positioned for your next as you eagerly anticipate what lies ahead.

CHAPTER 13
TRANSFORMATIVE TRANSITIONS AND ASSISTANCE

NOTHING HAPPENS until the pain of REMAINING THE SAME OUTWEIGHS the pain of CHANGE.[8]

ARTHUR BURT

Life transitions of change are transformative in essence. As you effectively navigate and negotiate the transitions of life, you will experience change. The degree of change depends largely on the trade-off and how much you are willing to work through. There are no short cuts to your next. As you are experiencing right now, you know it is costing you something to transition and transform. No cross, no crown! No pain, no gain!

Maya Angelou eloquently stated, "We delight in the beauty of the butterfly, but rarely admit the changes it has gone through to achieve

---

8   Arthur Burt, "Nothing happens until the pain of remaining the same outweighs the pain of change," *Wordpress.com*, https://developingsuperleaders.wordpress.com/2017/06/21/nothing-happens-until-the-pain-of-remaining-the-same-outweighs-the-pain-of-change-arthur-burt/.

that beauty."[9] Going through adversity and enduring our TRADEOFFS makes us even more POWERFUL than we already are. It makes us braver, stronger, and a more determined Nexter. A trade-off is a situational decision that involves diminishing or losing one quality, quantity, or property of a set or design in return for gains in other aspects. In simple terms, a tradeoff is where one thing increases, and another must decrease. We all make important decisions every day that involve trade-offs that impact not only *NEXTing* from our now to our next but brings with it the pain of transformation. When we make an important decision, we often have to accept the tradeoffs that come along with it. Tradeoffs typically come with physical and/or emotional discomfort. Accepting and working through tradeoffs contributes to our GOD-FIDENCE and builds our resilience. Everyone who wants to go from their present to their future must declare that the pain of remaining the same outweighs the pain of change. Here are some LifeWork Principles that will help you transform as you transition regarding the trade-offs:

LWP #1: ACKNOWLEDGE THE TRADE-OFFS—Don't be naive or deceived—there is going to be a cost. "Then Jesus said to His disciples, 'If anyone desires to come after Me, let him deny himself, and take up his cross, and follow Me'" (Matthew 16:24, NKJV). There are no free tickets to success! You must acknowledge that if you remain the way that you are it is going to cost you more. And if you stay where you are it is going to hurt you more. You can't afford that, you must transform and transition to your next.

LWP #2: ACCEPT THE TRADE-OFFS—The key to personal growth, change, and development by way of the life transition is accepting trade-offs, which typically come with physical and/or emotional discomfort. There isn't a task that's important to us that isn't inclusive of a

---

9   Maya Angelou, "We delight in the beauty of the butterfly, but rarely admit the changes it has gone through to achieve that beauty," *goodreads*, https://www.goodreads.com/quotes/84834-we-delight-in-the-beauty-of-the-butterfly-but-rarely.

tradeoff. A tradeoff can be painful in the short term but is well worth it in the long term. It's the result of the challenge, adversity, and concerted effort that makes the accomplishment even more anticipated and sweeter.

During the week leading up to my life transition of change, I had to acknowledge and accept that there would be trade-offs. There would be some blood, sweat, and tears on the floor. I was going to pay the cost to get to my next. The pain of remaining the same far outweighed the pain of transformation and transition. I prayed, and I cried, and I cried, and I prayed all the while I was writing the letter of resignation.

LWP #3: WORKING THROUGH THE TRADE-OFFS— Working through the trade-offs is necessary for your success. Following through strengthens you throughout the process, albeit painful. Working through the painful trade-offs is good pain, you know, like the good pain you feel after exercise that is dull and achy. This is actually a good sign that your muscles are becoming stronger. So in working through the trade-offs on your way to your next, you are going to feel some good pain. It is worth it! You are worth it!

> **NEXT Notes:** It most often takes challenges to see change!

TRANSITION ASSISTANCE

When you judge yourself for needing help, you judge those you are helping. When you attach value to giving help, you attach value to needing help. The danger of tying your self-worth to being a helper is feeling shame when you have to ask for help. Offering help is courageous and compassionate, but so is asking for help.[10]*—Brené Brown*

---

10 Brené Brown, *Rising Strong: How the Ability to Reset Transforms the Way We Live, Love, Parent, and Lead* (Manhattan, NY: Random House Publishing Group, 2017), 180.

God does not want you to live on your pain; He wants you to live through your pain.

When did needing help and asking for it become a bad thing? I discovered that my transition and transformation were prolonged because I had masked my pain and did not ask for help. Getting help is not a bad thing! While *NEXTing*, pain can be a catalyst for getting started and persevering, but it must not become your daily food. God does not want you to live on your pain; He wants you to live through your pain. The writer of Psalm 42 talks about this in verses 1-5: (MSG):

I wonder, "Will I ever make it—arrive and drink in God's presence?" I'm on a diet of tears—tears for breakfast, tears for supper. All day long, people knock at my door, pestering, "Where is this God of yours?" These are the things I go over and over, emptying out the pockets of my life. I was always at the head of the worshiping crowd, right out in front, leading them all, eager to arrive and worship, shouting praises, singing thanksgiving—celebrating, all of us, God's feast! Why are you down in the dumps, dear soul? Why are you crying the blues?

Friend, this may be how you feel. I know it was for me when I was *NEXTing*. You may be wondering if you are going to make it through the life transition of change to your next. The tears associated with the pain of the change is your diet. While you are dealing with the transition, it feels like people are insensitive and are pressuring you. On the outside, you are trying to put up a good front, but inwardly you are down in the dumps and crying the blues. It is time to admit that you need HELP!

Navigating and negotiating the land in between your now and your next may require assistance. The first step is admitting that you need help! It is said that one of life's real tragedies is not needing help but needing help and not knowing that you need help. Again, it is okay if you are not okay. It's okay if you don't know what to do. Take a few moments and pray about who you can ask for help, and in humility, with courage, ask. We have not because we ask not. Even if it's professional help you need, ask! There is no shame in needing help. Stop judging yourself for needing help. Recognize the signs that you need assistance and go get help. It is courageous and wise to ask for help.

Don't pretend that all is well when you know that it isn't. *NEXTing* will help you navigate and negotiate, push through and past the guilt, shame, or condemnation you feel for needing help. If you don't know what you're doing, pray to the Father. He loves to help. You'll get God's help, and you won't be condescended to when you ask for it. Ask boldly and believingly without a second thought. People who "worry their prayers" are like wind-whipped waves. Don't think you're going to get anything from the Father that way, adrift at sea, keeping all your options open (see James 1:5-8). God wants to help you deal with the pain or fear that comes when you experience life's transitions so that you don't get stuck in the experience or lost in transition.

Secondly, it is vital to learn how to receive help. I am reminded of the times I have called for AAA roadside service. The representative scheduling your roadside assistance makes sure that you are ready to receive help. You must provide certain information pertaining to the type of assistance that you need. You must provide contact information and be present when the technician arrives to help. For me, this translates into admitting that you need help and that you want the help. Being present when the help arrives is key because it speaks to the attitude one must possess when receiving assistance. You must understand that you are the one receiving support; therefore, you don't have to know it all or judge yourself for requesting the help. Like travel, life transitions of change can be testing and hazardous at times.

nexting

Please be discerning when receiving help, because not all help is helpful. Receiving assistance requires patience and gratitude. As you are receiving aid, understand that the person is not there to unburden you with the responsibility of doing your part; they are there to help. When you welcome help during your transition, it makes *NEXTing* smoother, more efficient, and more effectual on a much deeper level. To receive the help that you need, remember why you requested help in the first place and keep reminding yourself of that reason. Make sure that the person giving you the help is not condemning, judgmental, or condescending. Receiving help does not mean that you are helpless and hopeless.

The final note about receiving help is that it is temporary. It is like the donut tires you get when you have a flat. When one of your tires goes out, it is replaced with a donut tire (also called a spare tire, although a spare tire is typically the same size as a regular tire). The donut tire is intended to provide you with a means of assisted mobility so you can get to the mechanic and have your tire changed as soon as possible. Donut tires are not meant to replace the original tire and to be driven on for long periods of time. They are temporary. When you perceive the help as temporary, though necessary, it will help you receive assistance as you are *NEXTing*. I would like to offer you several *NEXTing* tips for receiving helpful assistance as you navigate and negotiate life transitions of change:

Transitions and Changing Lanes

"So, change lanes. Get your stride back. Don't stay on a road that can only lead to further devastation."[11] Changing lanes is a part of navigating and negotiating the transitions of life. In *NEXTing*, changing lanes implies that you are making adjustments through the transition that allow for maximum results. Changing lanes helps you

---

11 Rita Zahara, "So, change lanes. Get your stride back. Don't stay on a road that can only lead to further devastation," *Quotefancy*, https://quotefancy.com/quote/1789787/Rita-Zahara-So-change-lanes-Get-your-stride-back-Don-t-stay-on-a-road-that-can-only-lead.

TRANSFORMATIVE TRANSITIONS AND ASSISTANCE

to gain momentum and continuity in life as go from now to next. When navigating through a transition, everyone has their own pace. Changing lanes during the transition allows you to adjust your speed while respecting the process. Adjusting your pace is a healthy way of maintaining your force, energy, or momentum to complete the change. For example, there are times that you need to slow the process down a little for a complete transformation and development of character to take place. Then, there are times you pick up the pace of the transition because you do not want to prolong the change unnecessarily. Maintaining momentum is critical for navigating and negotiating your transition—once it is broken, it is hard to duplicate all the factors involved in your transition and transformation.

Changing lanes speaks to your flexibility as a person who is open to growth, change, and development. Being flexible and open to change within the negotiating of your transition proves to be very helpful in creating continuity for yourself and others. There is preparation that goes into changing lanes, right? As in driving, *NEXTing* life's transitions requires preparation before making changes to maintain continuity amid the change. It helps you to be agile in thought and life. Certain aspects of *NEXTing* help you slow things down mentally so that you can evaluate all your options before making a significant decision. *NEXTing* assists you in looking at the big picture or the details of the selected route so that you may be patient in navigating and negotiating your transition. As you are navigating and negotiating from now to next, transformation is realized because *NEXTing* coaches you through the process of connecting the dots.

When changing lanes in life, you must be aware of your blind spots. If you change lanes without paying attention to your blind spots, you could be headed for a certain collision. "The highway of life was littered with the roadkill of those who didn't know when to change lanes."[12] Therefore, you change lanes carefully to avoid a collision with another motorist. So it is with life transitions; you have to navigate and negotiate the changes carefully to avoid making the severe mistake of colliding into someone else's emotions or issues. For example, when a family is dealing with the death of a loved one in the nucleus family, each member would do well to consider the other members' emotional states before making any major life decisions. Throughout the process of *NEXTing*, you are encouraged to maintain excellent communication with significant others who are *NEXTing* with you to expose your possible unconscious biases (blind spots). With open, courageous communication, the likelihood of addressing unconscious biases is increased, thus avoiding the blind spots and destructive collisions associated with making changes in life transitions and intersections.

Transitions and Delays

Whenever you travel, delays are a possibility. There are traffic delays. Traffic delay means the additional travel time experienced by a highway user due to conditions, incidents, and events including, but not limited to, road construction, maintenance activities, accidents, and avalanche closures. It is measured as the time difference between actual travel time and free-flow travel time. There are flight delays. A flight delay occurs when an airline flight takes off and/or lands later than its scheduled time. There is what is known as a transit delay. To put it simply, a transit delay means that the delivery is taking longer than usual due to many factors, such as weather delays, split shipments, or even a lost package. All of these forms of delays from travel to traffic to flight to transit speak to the understanding that in life transitions of change, it would be naïve and deceptive not to consider the possibility that as you next, you may

---

12   Karen White, *After the Rain (A Falling Home Novel)* (New York, NY: Berkley, 2012), 1.

experience some delays. Just because you are expecting, embracing, and experiencing *NEXTing* doesn't mean that you won't have to deal with delays. In fact, *NEXTing* is designed to equip you to anticipate the unexpected as well as the expected. When you are prepared, you don't have to panic just because there is some form of delay on the route that you have chosen to take to get to your next. Remember, *NEXTing* is the conscious anticipation of the plans of God unfolding in your life as you engage in the now.

Therefore, be confident and aware that God is not caught off guard when a delay is experienced along the way. Trust that God has planned for the delay. He can reschedule your transition or reroute your path towards your next.

Transitions and Destinations

Every transition has a point and place of destination. In the shipping industry, a place of destination refers to the agreed location to which a shipment is expected to arrive. When the shipment reaches its delivery point, then the carrier or transport company has fulfilled its delivery obligation. So it is in *NEXTing*. God has planned for your arrival at a particular destination, called your next. And when you get there, that chapter of your life has been accomplished and your next has become your now. Here is another perspective for you to consider when it comes to transitions and destinations. Google Maps and navigational systems require you to identify a destination point or place. This destination point becomes the point of reference to produce the best route for your travel. Now consider with me that God's unfolding plan for your destination point is your next and based upon what is next for you will now factor into the best route for you to get there. Sometimes the best route is not always straight ahead. Whichever route He has you take, you have to trust that it is the best route! Sometimes that route is different than others' routes who may be going to the same destination point.

nexting

In other words, your life transition of change may be totally different from someone else's. Whenever you open these apps, AI asks for two destination points; one is your current location, and the second your desired location. This can be likened to your now (your current location) and your next (your desired location). Did you know that you can even add multiple destinations? In life transitions of change, there may be multiple stops between your now and your next, or sometimes one life transition of change is immediately followed by another life transition of change, all leading towards your next.

Transitions and Detours

Caution: Detours ahead! There is a story in the Bible of a woman named Naomi who, along with one of her daughters-in-law, faced a life transition of change that blindsided them. This transition was the death of their respective husbands. *NEXTing* helps you navigate and negotiate these detours you encounter between your now and your next. The book of Ruth tells us the story of these women:

> *But Ruth said, "Do not urge me to leave you or to turn back from following you; for where you go, I will go, and where you lodge, I will lodge. Your people will be my people, and your God, my God."—Ruth 1:16 (AMP)*

> *Naomi said to her daughter-in-law, "May he be blessed of the LORD who has not ceased his kindness to the living and to the dead." Again Naomi said to her, "The man is one of our closest relatives, one who has the right to redeem us."—Ruth 2:20 (AMP)*

The *NEXTing* mindset and heart-set include always being open to growth, development, and change, even when you are going through unforeseen adversity. Difficult detours do not mean you have to cancel the journey. When you are *NEXTing*, sometimes another life transition of change happens inside of the current life transition of change. "Life be lifeing," right? But because you are *NEXTing*, you are already prepared through mental toughness and internal fortitude to continue to effectively navigate and negotiate the detours in the life transitions of change. Even if your detours have detours, you are going to be okay and get where you are going!

> **NEXT Notes:** In the life transitions of change, your detours can have detours. But *NEXTing* helps you effectively navigate and negotiate difficult detours.

Transitions and Distance

"Are we there yet?" These four words are often heard on a road trip or any form of travel, for that matter. They express the anticipated excitement of finally reaching the planned destination, as well as the frustration associated with the length of travel and the amount of distance left before arriving at the designated destination. When you are *NEXTing* through the in-between, don't allow the deficits you experience along the way destroy to your dreams. Don't allow the distance you have traveled and the amount of distance left to travel to discourage you from pressing through. And finally, don't allow the distance in the life transitions of change between your now and your next to become the focus of the journey. Remember the journey is just as important as the destination.

Transitions and Exits

When navigating and negotiating life's transitions of change, God is always faithful to provide us with exits. On road trips, exits serve the purpose of allowing us to take new roads and go in new directions. Sometimes, your life transition of change is God's provision for you to choose a new route. Along the highways we travel, the posted exit signs inform us about the distance left to go before reaching them. These signs also identify markers so that you can distinguish one exit from another. *NEXTing* incorporates the purposes of exits into its process. For example, it is helpful to be able to discern between good and best when it comes to your options. *NEXTing* encourages you throughout your transition period to persevere through the distance until you reach the best exit.

Exits also serve as the access points to your desired destinations. First Corinthians 10:13 (MSG) says this: "No test or temptation that comes your way is beyond the course of what others have had to face. All you need to remember is that God will never let you down; he'll never let you be pushed past your limit; he'll always be there to help you come through it." It is essential to know that there is an access point to your desired destination when you are *NEXTing* through a painful transition in life. God is present with you, helping you come through rough transitions and arrive at the right exit. Many people think the sole purpose of an exit sign is to mark stairwells and building exits. The real function of LED exit signs is to allow you to find the exit or emergency route in the event of an emergency. *NEXTing* bolsters the joy of change as you anticipate an access point to your desired destination. Exits are necessary, celebrated, and valued in *NEXTing*. When is your next exit ahead?

Transitions and Fuel and Charging Stations

"A [consistently] righteous man hates lying and deceit, but a wicked man is loathsome [his very breath spreads pollution] and he comes [surely] to shame" (Proverbs 13:5, AMPC). The effectiveness of *NEXTing* is impacted by what is fueling it. When facing a life transition of change or attempting to make a life transition of change, you must have enough drive to get results. Desiring change is not enough; you must have purposed determination that translates into sustainable action and follow-through. Ambition is an ardent desire to achieve a particular end. But ambition alone is not enough. When *NEXTing*, you must have the fuel or the energy to sustain the ambitious goal or desire. The fuel or energy to go the distance is your purposed determination. Fill up or charge up by staying connected to your purpose.

Another interesting note is that fueling stations and charging stations are strategically placed along the highways of your life journey. Keep a careful eye on your fuel level or charge level, for they tell you how much fuel and energy you have or don't have. *NEXTing* helps you to keep your eyes on the goal, where God is beckoning you. Do you have this kind of drive and diligence? Do you have enough fuel in your tank or charge in storage to make the life transition of change?

> **NEXT Notes:** NO WHY, NO GO! If you don't know your "why," you should not be doing it. Your "why" is your purpose.

Something else to consider when talking about fuel and energy for the life transition of change is having the right fuel in your tank or a quality charge. What happens when your motive is wrong? Operating a motor vehicle using the wrong fuel type or having a poor power connection is hazardous and will produce unfavorable results. So it is with life transitions of change. When your motive is wrong for the transition, you will produce unfavorable results. For example, unhealthy motives (those that degrade the human condition in ourselves or others) are not good fuel for driving through your transition. *NEXTing* frowns upon unhealthy motives being the impetus behind your transition. Unhealthy motives could be hurting you. They are not sustainable and produce stress and inconsistency. Unhealthy motives speak to your current state of being and even your character. If you are facing a transition with unhealthy motives, ask yourself, "Is this the kind of person I am? Is this who I want to be?" If the answer is no, reexamine your motives and make the necessary changes before you proceed.

Transitions and Holding Patterns

There are times when you are experiencing a life transition of change when you will encounter a purposeful pause before proceeding forward. In *NEXTing*, this purposeful pause functions like a holding pattern. A holding pattern is the flight path maintained by an aircraft awaiting permission to land. It is a maneuver designed to delay an aircraft already in flight while keeping it within a specified airspace. For example, if you are going through the life transition of a career switch, *NEXTing* will help you navigate and negotiate the period between one career and the next by way of a purposeful pause. In this instance, the purposeful pause may be a time in which you are developing or enhancing your skills by going back to school or taking some training courses related to your new career. What you must determine and decide is if you are staying stuck somewhere you don't belong. Are you stuck, or simply in a holding pattern?

In *NEXTing*, a purposeful pause is not a period of no progress or change.

Another example is the life transition from singlehood to marriage. When it comes to love at first sight, *NEXTing* doesn't encourage you to jump into a marriage. *NEXTing* coaches you into several purposeful pauses known as friendship, courtship, engagement, and then marriage. In *NEXTing*, a purposeful pause is not a period of no progress or change. There is still progress and transformation taking place inside of you—and even around you—that will impact your next. During this purposeful pause, God is developing your character to coincide with your next. Simultaneously, He is preparing things around your anticipated arrival in your future.

Remember, *NEXTing* assists you in avoiding stasis and stagnation. Stay woke; there is not a day that goes by that the unfolding grace of God is not taking place in your life. The night is about over; dawn is about to break. Be up and awake to what God is doing! He is putting the finishing touches on you as you transition through your now to your next. We can't afford to waste a minute—we must not squander these precious daylight hours. Stay ready and attentive, because your holding pattern could break any moment now!

When the holding pattern has been lifted, the aircraft is permitted to land; so it is with *NEXTing*. When the purposeful pause has been removed, you have divine permission to pursue what is next. "For surely there is a latter end [a future and a reward], and your hope and expectation shall not be cut off" (Proverbs 23:18, AMPC). While you are in your purposeful pause, your hope and expectation are not being diminished—in fact, they are growing.

Transitions and the In-Between

"They found grace out in the desert, these people who survived the killing. Israel, out looking for a place to rest, met God out looking for them" (Jeremiah 31:2, MSG)! Wow, this is a tremendous thought to keep in mind when you are navigating and negotiating life transitions of change; when you are out there experiencing it all and life gets rough along the way, you can find grace in the wilderness, or better yet, grace will find you! There were times where grace found me through an encouraging word or gesture by someone I knew or a stranger. I recall after I submitted my letter of resignation and stepped into my next that God's grace found me through a friendship that was created with a local Bible bookstore vendor, Ruby Wheeler. A part of my next was the founding of a new ministry and like all new ministries or ventures, capital was at a premium, but God! Ruby sought me out on two occasions to bless and sow into our ministry with financial gifts in the thousands of dollars. Friend, while you are out looking for a place to rest, you will meet God who is out looking for you! The favor of your next is looking for you to stay the course during the land in-between and thereafter. Don't get in a rush, but employ patience as you are experiencing the life transition of change so that you come through the transition whole and lacking nothing.

Transitions and Rest Stops

Rest stops are located right off interstate highways (you can see them from the road) and are meant for people to pull in and rest if they're tired, sleepy, or fatigued. The rest area's primary role is to enhance traffic safety by reducing crash incidents on the roadway. Rest stops have places to walk and enjoy nature, restrooms to relieve yourself, restaurants to replenish yourself, gas stations and charging stations, and places to get information. As you navigate and negotiate life transitions of change, take advantage of the rest stops along the way. The utilization of resting can be seen as a part of the navigation and negotiation of the life transition of change. Learn to embrace the concept of rest and incorporate it into your life regularly. So many people are going through their life transitions of change exhausted, burned out, weary, and running on empty. You can do something about that in your own life, you can start to use the rest stops that grace provides for you along the journey between your now and your next. You can also show that you care about others on their journeys to use the rest stops that grace provides for them.

Transitions and Tolls

It is going to cost you something to travel towards your next. Friend, the Bible teaches us in Luke 14:28-30 (AMPC),

> *For which of you, wishing to build a farm building, does not first sit down and calculate the cost [to see] whether he has sufficient*

means to finish it? Otherwise, when he has laid the foundation and is unable to complete the building, all who see it [the building] will begin to mock and jeer at him, saying, this man began to build and was not able (worth enough) to finish.

From money to time to emotions, you are going to have to pay the price of effectively navigating and negotiating life transitions.

Like taking road trips, certain roads have a toll attached to them. And if you want to take a particular route, you're going to have to pay the toll. When we apply this to *NEXTing*, we understand that it is going to cost you to travel from now to next. All of life's transitions come with an expense. It would help if you considered the cost associated with going from where you are now to where you want to be next. Even when you're dealing with an unexpected or sudden life transition, there is a cost. The costs associated with life transitions are both tangible and intangible. From money to time to emotions, you are going to have to pay the price of effectively navigating and negotiating life transitions. Remember what I shared with you about the trade-offs. In *NEXTing*, a trade-off can be likened to a toll.

Let me ask you a few questions:

Do you know the cost up-front that is connected to the life transition of change you are taking?

How prepared are you to pay for the life transition of change you desire?

What are you doing to prepare for the transition between your now and your next?

How much relationship capital do you have in place to absorb the cost of unexpected and expected life transitions of change?

For that matter, do you have a rainy-day savings account to absorb the cost of a sudden life transition?

I'm glad that I have you thinking—and hopefully preparing for—the tolls associated with life transitions. *NEXTing* emphasizes the importance of preparedness to effectively navigate and negotiate life's transitions.

Transitions in Transitions

"The next years are going to see a total drought—not a drop of dew or rain unless I say otherwise." God then told Elijah, "Get out of here, and fast. Head east and hide out at the Kerith Ravine on the other side of the Jordan River. You can drink fresh water from the brook; I've ordered the ravens to feed you." Elijah obeyed God's orders. He went and camped in the Kerith canyon on the other side of the Jordan. And sure enough, ravens brought him his meals, both breakfast and supper, and he drank from the brook. Eventually the brook dried up because of the drought. Then God spoke to him: "Get up and go to Zarephath in Sidon and live there. I've instructed a woman who lives there, a widow, to feed you."—1 Kings 17:1-9, MSG)

Life is filled with transitions—and swift transitions, at that. Life transitions of change occur within other life transitions of change. It is not surprising that, while you are navigating and negotiating through one change, another one presents itself and demands your attention. No need to despair; *NEXTing* prepares you to effectively navigate and negotiate all changes in front of you. I remember a time when I was *NEXTing* through my life transition of resigning from my first pastorate and beginning my second ministry. It was during this time that my family and I had to deal with the home foreclosure I mentioned earlier. That experience taught me so much about *NEXTing*.

God gave me the revelation that we were experiencing home foreclosure, for-closure. It was during the Great Recession that there was an economic decline in world markets for the period of 2007-2009. I walked away from that experience knowing that certain things happen in our lives so that we can have closure. Inside of *NEXTing*, each life transition has an ending and a beginning. The transition that occurs inside of the original transition does not have to derail you or stop your momentum; it merely needs to be addressed and continue moving forward.

In *NEXTing*, I liken the subject of transitions inside of transitions to several driving scenarios. When driving, there are times you have to merge with traffic to arrive at your desired destination. While it may be ideal to travel on the road all by yourself, it is highly unlikely— therefore, merges are to be expected. So it is in life: having to address another life transition while already living through one is to be expected.

Speaking of merging while driving, the skill of yielding comes into play. In road transport, a "yield" or "give way" sign indicates that merging drivers must prepare to stop if necessary to let a driver approach or proceed. A driver who stops or slows down to let another vehicle through has yielded the right of way to that vehicle. To effectively navigate and negotiate through life transitions, one needs to incorporate the skill of yielding to the right mindset and heart-set. Just because you have to yield to confront a life change inside of another life change does not mean that you won't get to where you intend to go. Trust me—you will be all right!

Switching lanes is another analogy. It would be best if you changed lanes when you present as a danger to yourself and others by being in another lane. This may include situations such as going too slow in the "fast lane" or going too fast in the "slow lane." In life's transitions, sometimes you should venture into another transition to navigate through the first. While we were going through the home foreclosure, we immediately moved into a condo for a few months because it later became uncomfortably safe; therefore, we had to move again for the safety of my family. Eventually, by switching lanes inside of the life transition of home foreclosure, we arrived at a condo that we gratefully called home for several years.

Keep your eyes on the big picture when dealing with transitions inside of transitions. Though you may be merging, yielding, and switching lanes, you are still on the road toward the desired destination. And *NEXTing* helps you formulate this perspective so that you can maintain the continuity necessary to navigate and negotiate life's transitions effectively.

Transitions and Turbulence

Tribulations will accompany life's transitions of change. Sometimes, tribulation sparks the transition. I also refer to tribulations in transition as turbulence. When the pilot comes over the speaker to advise the crew and passengers, he often says that he is turning on the seatbelt sign and he needs everyone to be seated, because the aircraft is flying through some, (wait for it), turbulence.

Turbulence is expected. Turbulence can be embraced. You will experience turbulence. When you are in transitional turbulence, return to your seat. Buckle up. Normal activity will be momentarily discontinued. Ride it out. Know that you will pass through it, and the turbulence will eventually be behind you. Normal activity will resume. Turbulence does not stop you from getting to your destination.

There's more to come: we continue to shout our praise even when we're hemmed in with troubles, because we know how troubles can develop passionate patience in us, and how that patience, in turn, forges the tempered steel of virtue, keeping us alert for whatever God will do next. In alert expectancy such as this, we're never left feeling shortchanged. Quite the contrary—we can't round up enough containers to hold everything God generously pours into our lives through the Holy Spirit!—Romans 5:3-5 (MSG)

Transitions and Turns

The sudden and unexpected blindside in life transitions of change can be likened to the turns inside the transition. Something unexpected happens, it is going down, and you must deal with it. When *NEXTing*, making adjustments and remaining agile will be two of your best qualities. "Adapt on the fly" is a phrase used to describe a person who is good at making the necessary adjustments. First, there could be a situation when, during the life transition of change, you get news that something unexpected that you had not prepared for has occurred. What do you do? You adjust on the fly; you switch your game plan. When you adjust and make a couple of extra turns rather than complain and refuse to respond with a positive attitude, eventually you get to where you intend to go. Pay attention to how you deal with the need to make turns in your life transitions of change.

How you respond to each turn will impact your future. Learn to adjust to the sudden, unexpected turns. This means maintaining a consistent attitude as you embrace the unexpected. *NEXTing* teaches you to govern your response with the understanding that what you are experiencing is temporal. God has a plan for you, and He is going to finish what He started. God knows us far better than we know ourselves; He recognizes our potential, and He preserves us through the sudden turns.

An interesting note about transitions and turns is that turns can be quite revealing. Sudden turns can be just what you needed to arrive at your desired destination. There are times when a turn points you in the right direction. Sometimes, the life transition of change itself is the turn. Turns show you who is really with you. Sudden shifts become the excuses people use for walking away. Then there are the "U-turns" in life transitions of change. Please know that they are allowed. If the direction that your life is headed is not where you want it to go, pivot and make a U-turn. U-turns are necessary when what you see up ahead does not afford wise passage—when you are traveling in wrong directions because of pride or misinformation. These are no justifiable reasons to keep going. You know it's insane to keep doing the same thing over and over and expecting different results., and *NEXTing* will help you with that.

Transitions and Voice Navigation

Don't let the noise of others' opinions drown out your own inner voice. And most importantly, have the courage to follow your heart and intuition. Your inner voice can provide you with much needed calm and perspective to guide you forward to your next. Your inner voice can help with impulse control. Most of us have experienced it before. That little voice in our heads that tells us not to take that last slice of pizza, to "keep going" for that few extra minutes on the treadmill, or not to make that snippy comment that we desperately want to blurt out to our co-worker. Intuitively, we have a sense that we can tell ourselves what to do or talk ourselves out of something. But, does our inner voice really aid self-control and help us resist temptation? Yes, when it is not given to hubris.

On another note, the AI voice of the navigational systems during travel is extremely important. The AI voice is likened unto the voice of your next blending harmoniously with your inner voice, giving you needful guidance and motivational self-talk. During every waking moment, we carry on an inner dialogue. Whether you call it inner speech, self-talk, internal dialogue, or thinking to yourself, it seems to be an important part of our daily life. Even though most of these inner dialogues stay well hidden (except for the occasionally embarrassing moment), inner speech is far more important than most people realize.

From early childhood onward, inner speech plays a vital role in regulating how we think and behave during life transitions of change. Not only does it often allow us to "rehearse" different scenarios and enable us to avoid rash actions, but inner speech (voice navigation) can shape how we see the world around us, how we reframe our past, and look towards our future. For this reason, inner speech plays an important role in self-awareness and self-understanding, which is always good for life transitions of change.

A transformational transition is a transition that not only changes places and spaces, but you.

If you lock in, focus, and truly embrace your life transitions of change, they can become transformational and not just transactional. A transactional transition is simply going from one place to another, like simply moving from one house to another house. Transactional transitions can be stepping out of one line into another line. Transactional transitions can be ordinary and shallow in experience. Transactional transitions can also be limiting and confining. Just because you change zip codes or addresses or hairstyles or clothing doesn't mean that you have experienced a true-life transition of change. It is superficial at best, and will probably be temporal.

On the other hand, life transitions of change can be transformational as well as transitional. I believe that life transitions of change are meant to be transformational and transitional. When you experience a life transition of change from an embracing, authentic, and genuinely faithful mindset and heart-set, it will transform you!

A transformational transition is a transition that not only changes places and spaces but you. That is my prayer and hope for you as I write this book, share this information, and tell my story as I walk with you through this process that I call *NEXTing*. I want you to experience a transformational transition. *NEXTing* is the conscious anticipation of the unfolding plans of God as you engage in now, right? Well, what's going to make your life transition of change transformational? What is going to make the transition that you're going through transformational? I'm glad you asked! Your knowledge, your understanding, and your expectation should be that the transition is going to make you a different person. As you *NEXTing*, your thoughts, feelings, and choices change. Who you were before the life transition is not who you will be after the transition. It is like moving from one house to another house; the two homes are not going to be the same. The house is the same, but the occupant, the person, or the family residing in the new home is going to be different from the person or family that resided in it before they vacated or moved out. The person or family that turns the house into a home is different. In the same way, when you fully embrace and experience the life transition of change, you will be changed. Transformed from the inside out. Let it be new! Did you hear what I said? "let it be new," or better yet, "let you be new!" In your next, be new. Be older, be more mature, be wiser, be stronger, be kinder—just BE NEW! NEXT IS NEW! And I think that your next deserves a new you! How about that?

> ***NEXT Notes:*** Next is new! Let it be new! Let you be new, Too!

CHAPTER 14
NEXT IS NOW

"Rather than indulging in whatever strikes our momentary fancy, we take responsibility for the welfare of our future selves."[13]

DANIEL GILBERT

When you input your destination into Google Maps or some other GPS, the computer calculates several route options. It provides estimated times of arrival based on current traffic conditions, construction, detours, posted speed limits, and the type of route chosen (shortest in terms of distance, fastest in terms of time, etc.). Once locked in, your driving route gives you audible and visual promptings at every turn toward your desired destination. The audio and visual prompts are influenced by your desired destination. Thus, your ultimate destination has an impact on your current and progressive steps. Where you want to be in the future will cause you to make critical decisions in your present. It is like what I shared with you earlier about having the "next" on the side of the basketball court. Whoever has next assumes earnest responsibility for what is currently going on in the present. Your next

---
13 Daniel Gilbert, *Stumbling on Happiness* (Vintage, 2007), 14-15.

becomes a significant influencer of your now. Your future self demands a certain quality of attention and care for your current self.

> **NEXT Notes:** Next is now: Your next is the great influencer of your now.

The "Next is Now" idea suggests that in the here and now—right now—you have clear choices before you, some grave, some hopeful, and some just plain thoughtless. You are not an animal limited to instincts, short in options, and without the wherewithal to alter decisions. We are humans guided by evidential reasoning powers—often called common sense—that should always be conscious of the time beyond the current. Yes, we live in the now with collective rational powers to change the fast-coming future. Therefore, there is a direct connection between the next you desire, the current actions that you take, and the choices you make in the now.

NEXTing helps you to understand that when engage in the now and live with the conscious anticipation of God's plans unfolding in your life, you underscore a future orientation to enhance your choices and behavior in your now. You are a future-oriented human living in the now. This is so helpful when it comes to making decisions because they will impact your future when you arrive there now.

What are you dreaming or thinking about doing right now that might take some time to come to fruition? Are you working on something? Are you considering something big? Here's the bottom line: the future is coming, and there's nothing you can do to stop it. Use this knowledge to become a better steward of your present. *NEXTing* helps you acknowledge the vision of God's good and valid plans for your future now. *NEXTing* incorporates both vision and faith.

NEXTing helps you seize the opportunity of a lifetime while there is life in the opportunity.

Imagination and faith help you to see a future for yourself and, by faith, bring it into your present. *NEXTing* helps you actualize what is calling out to you from your vision of the future! Friend, whatever God showed you about your future may take some time and work. Worthy goals usually do. You can either take action now, accomplish those dreams, and enjoy the rewards, or you can put them off for five years because they take too long to achieve. Proverbs 13:12 (NKJV) says, "Hope deferred makes the heart sick; but when the desire comes, it is a tree of life." Next is now. You can put an end to the heart sickness associated with deferred dreams and begin to experience a productive and profitable life. You get to decide by allowing your next to direct your now.

> *NEXT Notes:* Next is N.O.W. (No opportunity waits!) Seize your NEXT NOW. *NEXTing* helps you seize the opportunity of a lifetime while there is life in the opportunity.

You are now tuned in to *NEXTing*. Envision your future now. Embrace the moment. Go out and make it happen. Make it happen for the kingdom, your family, your business, and—most of all—for you. It's your Kingdom destiny, and it is accessible today.

Next is now – don't bring your past into your future but bring your future into your present. Start now by seeing your future as reachable, realistic, and relational. Commence! *NEXTing* assists you in seeing that "next is now" is an opportunity to contemplate the transition to

nexting

something new in the future—right now! "Commencement" literally means the start of something new, now!

The tension with next comes because when people consider starting something new, they often have mixed feelings. Some piece of them wants to hold on to the old. (Every high school or college grad has felt this emotion—it is part of why alumni return for reunions.) For most people facing a life transition of change, the old feels safe, familiar, and comfortable—it's what they already know and are used to. It is part of their identity ("I'm a college student") and they know how to respond to any situation they are likely to encounter while there. In contrast, anything new, though it may come with the excitement of possibility, involves risk, and humans are naturally risk-averse. There is a bias to hold onto the old—even if that isn't always the best choice. In short, we all tend to "prefer the devil we know to the devil we don't". But "next is now" leads you past this conundrum into the future.

In baseball, the first step to stealing second base is to take your foot off first base! You can't do one without the other. Similarly, in life, to do things in a new way, you must first let go of your old way of doing things. To get to next, you have to let go of now. That is where most people get hung up, and it is one place where getting feedback from an outside observer or accountability partner can be helpful. Yet even when the advice to change comes from a good friend or another trusted source, most people don't want to hear it. *NEXTing* understands the truth that it takes immense effort to learn to do things in a new way, let alone to turn that new way into a new habit. But this is precisely what "next is now" in *NEXTing* addresses, so turning that new way into a new habit is organic and natural. Stop making excuses and start making changes because you are *NEXTing*, and next is now! Who among us has the kind of time and energy to do this? Especially when stressed or pressed for time (which is also when it's most critical), we tend to do what's familiar and comfortable—leaving change for: "Mmm . . . maybe later."

As you begin to see that next is now, you will learn to reprioritize time and not waste it in your now.

> **NEXT Notes:** Your next is connected to your now.

And Ruth said, "urge me not to leave you or to turn back from following you; for where you go, I will go, and where you lodge, I will lodge. Your people shall be my people and your God my God."—Ruth 1:16 (AMP)

And Naomi said to her daughter-in-law, "blessed be he of Lord who has not ceased his kindness to the living and to the dead." And Naomi said to her, "the man is a near relative of ours, one who has the right to redeem us."—Ruth 2:20 (AMP)

In *NEXTing*, you must recognize that your next is always connected to your now. In most instances, your future impacts how you handle your now. Where you want to be tomorrow affects your actions today. What you want to do next should influence your decisions now.

The plans God had for Ruth's and Naomi's next connected to their now. Naomi was bitter because she felt that her future as a widow was bleak. A grim outlook on her future compelled her to advise her daughter-in-law not to travel with her. However, Ruth was motivated out of love to follow and submit to Naomi. Ruth wanted to serve the God of Naomi. God had plans to prosper them and not to harm them, plans to give them hope and a future! God had arranged for their next to be different than their now. Naomi recognized this when she became aware that the man who was interested in Ruth was their kinsman-redeemer, Boaz. Enlightened with this information, she advised Ruth how to properly steward the affairs of her now based upon the potential and prosperity of their next. Ruth excellently followed the instructions of Naomi regarding serving Boaz. Boaz, in turn, according to the plan of God, redeemed Ruth and Naomi. Ruth's and Naomi's next became their now as they engaged in taking responsibility for the welfare of their future selves in their present.

I challenge you to allow your anticipated next to become the schoolmaster of your now. See your future through the lenses of vision and faith, coupled with corresponding action, until it becomes your now. Your next becomes your now the moment you take the first step of responsibility for it. For example, the moment you step on the court and start playing the game for which you had "next" is the moment it becomes the game of your now. Therefore, because you have a scheduled next on your calendar, it behooves you to be a faithful custodian of it today. This is why I say next is now.

If we lived with an understanding of *NEXTing*, we would do things differently in the present because we expect our lives to continue and for us to participate in our future. Perhaps we would strive to eat more consciously. We would become more socially mindful of how we entertain strangers. Rather than indulging in irresponsible, disconnected activities as if they had no consequences on the future, we would take responsibility for the well-being of our hopeful next. We would, in ant-like fashion, engage in the storehouse discipline of our finances each month so that we can enjoy our retirements on a putting green. If we live with an understanding of *NEXTing*, we would engage in disciplines of preparation for our expected tomorrows. In practice, *NEXTing* suggests that our future selves will benefit from the sacrifices, intelligent decisions, and the dietary forbearance of our present selves.[14] (Our Future Selves, Maria Popova).

God is investing in you for your change, growth, and development. Through faith and the *NEXTing* mindset and heart-set, you can experience your next now as now gives way to next. Next is the open door that has been opened for you by God, your faithfulness in the present, some person you have encountered, or a life event that you have experienced.

---

14 Maria Popova

BE OPEN TO THE NEXT MOVE OF GOD

They arrived at the place to which God had directed him. Abraham built an altar. He laid out the wood. Then he tied up Isaac and laid him on the wood. Abraham reached out and took the knife to kill his son. Just then an angel of God called to him out of Heaven, "Abraham! Abraham!" "Yes, I'm listening." "Don't lay a hand on that boy! Don't touch him! Now I know how fearlessly you fear God; you didn't hesitate to place your son, your dear son, on the altar for me." Abraham looked up. He saw a ram caught by its horns in the thicket. Abraham took the ram and sacrificed it as a burnt offering instead of his son.—Genesis 22:9-13 (MSG)

In *NEXTing*, you can't be stubborn with your thoughts. If you fall in love with your thoughts, you can delay your next. You become endeared to the thoughts of yesterday and hold onto them, preventing yourself from moving forward into your future. Therefore, we must be careful to use the wisdom of God when we have to shift suddenly so as not to become fearful and freeze. Be in tune with and familiar with God's voice to eliminate the possibility of disconnection from the preceding word of God. It helps to keep your inner ears open and your antennas up, because God is always talking.

When God told Abraham to offer up his son, Isaac, Abraham was ready to slay him. Suddenly, there was a voice that called out to him and told him to SHIFT! What if Abraham had shut down and developed an attitude with God because of what He asked him to do in the first place? He would have missed the second call, in which God provided the ram as the substitute for Isaac. In *NEXTing*, you must stay in tune with God through prayer and listening. Stay in tune with the Spirit of God until the voice of God leads into the manifestation of your next. Keep your frequency open and don't close your ears. Remaining open to God is important. He is shifting you into His perfect will and plan for your life—into your next.

Anticipating the not yet—what is on the horizon—is part of your DNA; therefore, keep your head up and look forward. There is more in front of you than behind you.

One of the critical motivations of *NEXTing* is the belief that you never stop growing. *NEXTing* helps you collaborate with the various transitions of life and live them out in a very practical way with the faith that all things work together for the good of those who love God and are called according to His purposes (see Romans 8:28). In other words, *NEXTing* sees life's transitions as passageways through which your evolving being is realized. *NEXTing* helps you cultivate a mental attitude and perspective that considers all transitions as portals through which you pass on your way to fulfilling the plans and purposes of God for your life. Thriving in your next is about the climb of the mountain, not the summit of the mountain.

> **NEXT Notes:** Be careful when setting goals, because we set goals for the people we are when we set them rather than the people we become when we reach them.

When you are thriving in *NEXTing*, you are moving and growing. Stasis or stagnation is where you stop growing. With God, there is always more to be and to do. The Bible says in Philippians 1:6 (AMPC), "And I am convinced and sure of this very thing, that He Who began a good work in you will continue until the day of Jesus Christ [right up to the time of His return], developing [that good work] and perfecting and bringing it to full completion in you." You see, when you are in step with the rhythms of grace, you know that you are a work in process, under construction.

NEXTing helps you thrive in life's transitions because you see them as rest stops and not destinations. It is not that you never achieve; it's not that you never accomplish things or complete projects—it is just that you know that there is more to do. Now don't get me wrong; in *NEXTing*, you are to recognize and celebrate your achievements, accomplishments, completions, and successes, but don't let success become your enemy. Life's transitions are stops along the journey of life. You stop long enough to enjoy and appreciate where you are and how far you have come, but you keep moving and growing.

CHAPTER 15
TOWARDS

"We thrive not when we've done it all, but when we still have more to do."[15]
SARAH LEWIS

Hey, Nexter, did you know that you still have more to do? "Towards" indicates that you have not arrived and that you are in constant motion moving in the direction of the unfolding plans of God for your life. Towards is acknowledging that the only constant in life is change and God will have you well on your way, reaching out to lay hold of that perfection or mastery within the transition, knowing that you cannot really reach perfection in this life, but your goal is to "press on" as if it were attainable.

The secret to success is longevity. And the secret to longevity is managing continuity and change. How do we manage continuity and change as we transition? We do it by *NEXTing*! We learn to effectively navigate and negotiate life transitions of change. Although there are

---

15 Sarah Lewis, "We thrive not when we've done it all, but when we still have more to do," *A-Z Quotes*, https://www.azquotes.com/quote/1247892.

disruptions in life, there are built-in systems and structures in your life that will help you.

Towards is knowing what to change and what to continue. Because if you change what you should continue, you will lose your identity. And if you continue what you should change, you will become irrelevant. Remember, *NEXTing* is the unfolding plans of God being experienced in reality as you navigate and negotiate life's transitions. Knowing what to keep and what to let go of is played out in towards.

In golf, you adjust your towards from hole to hole. Your "towards" at hole number ten may be different than your towards at hole number three depending on the design of that particular hole and the distance between the tee and the hole itself.

BEING AND BECOMING

In *NEXTing*, you can grow deeper and broader during a particular life transition. For example, once you get married, you don't jump out of that marriage and move on to another. You and your spouse commit to not allow stasis and stagnation to define that marriage. What do you do in that marriage? You KEEP GROWING! You and your spouse grow more rooted and broader in love, knowledge, understanding, experiences, and so on. You are *NEXTing* in your marriage when you understand that you are to keep growing. You have not only survived the different ups and downs that marriage brings, but you thrive inside of your marriage because there is more to be and do! You get it, don't you? Succeeding in your next is about mastery.

NEXTing towards mastery means moving towards self-actualization. Maslow explicitly defines self-actualization to be "the desire for self-fulfillment, namely the tendency for him [the individual] to become actualized in what he is potentially." This tendency is phrased as the desire to become more and more what one is—to become everything that one is capable of becoming. As you effectively navigate and negotiate life's transitions, you are discovering and mastering your fullest potential in that particular transition. A more explicit definition of self-actualization, according to Maslow, is "intrinsic growth of what is already in the organism, or more accurately of what is the organism itself. Self-actualization is growth-motivated rather than deficiency-motivated." In *NEXTing*, you are being and becoming your authentic self.

"Human beings are works in progress that mistakenly think they're finished. The person you are right now is as transient, as fleeting and as temporary as all the people you've ever been. The one constant in our lives is change."[16] As a Nexter, you realize that you are in progress, evolving and growing to fit the future plans that God has for you. Through your life experiences and life transitions of change, you are moving towards the mastery and best version of you.

I hope this book has helped you see that, as living beings, we are not finished, and our life transitions are not the final acts of our lives. We are works in progress because God is not finished with us. *Nexting* begins with the understanding that God has thoughts about us and plans for us. It is His thoughts about us that define our being and not the life transitions that we have had or will have. It is God's plans for us that give life and shape to our being and becoming. God has not given the power and authority of our being and becoming to a specific experience in life. He uses life transitions to reveal to us His thoughts, plans, and purposes for our being and becoming.

As you earnestly engage in *NEXTing*, you discover that the various transitions of life, though painful, are essential to your growth and development as a person. You are a living, spiritual being that has a soul and possesses a body with thoughts, plans, and purposes that God has ordained for your life. It is through the portals of life's transitions

---

16 Gilbert, *Stumbling on Happiness*, 14-15.

that you acquire the freedom and opportunity to discover, express, and share your being and becoming with the rest of the living world. In philosophy, becoming is the possibility of change in a thing that has being—a thing that exists.

In *NEXTing*, not only are you transitioning from now to next, but you are also transforming from being to becoming.

In the philosophical study of ontology, the concept of "becoming" originated in ancient Greece from the philosopher Heraclitus of Ephesus, who, in the sixth century B.C., said that nothing in this world is constant except change and becoming. Heraclitus made this point with the famous quote, "No man ever steps in the same river twice."[17] The reason for this is that the river is moving, and you are moving. When you step in a river for the first time and later go back and step in the same river again, the body of water—and you—are different than the first time. The whole flows as a river, and as everything flows, nothing stands still. So, it is with you and *NEXTing*: each transition in life, even if many of them are similar, gives you an opportunity to be and become. Who you are in your now will be different than who you are in your next because you are becoming. In *NEXTing*, not only are you transitioning from now to next, but you are also transforming from being to becoming. Life's transitions help you to shed the old you and embrace and be the new you post-transition.

The concept of "becoming" connects with movement, growth, and development. Becoming assumes a "changing to" and a "moving

---

17 Heraclitus, "No man ever steps in the same river twice," *BrainyQuote*, https://www.brainyquote.com/quotes/heraclitus_107157.

toward." Becoming is the process or state of change—coming about in time and space.

A fundamental misconception about life's transitions and our transformation are that we think we arrive. At any point along our journey, we tend to believe that who we are at that moment is the final destination of our becoming. This, of course, is not only wrong but a source of much of our unhappiness. *NEXTing* says that your now is not your final destination because there is a God-ordained next in your future. It says who you are now does not define you, because God is at work within you, transforming you into who you are becoming next. In *NEXTing*, being and becoming is explained by the words of the Apostle Paul:

> *And all of us, as with unveiled face, [because we] continued to behold [in the Word of God] as in a mirror the glory of the Lord, are constantly being transfigured into His very own image in ever increasing splendor and from one degree of glory to another; [for this comes] from the Lord [Who is] the Spirit.—2 Corinthians 3:18 (AMPC)*

Understanding the Bible and being able to apply it to your everyday life is a critical part of *NEXTing*. The Bible functions as your compass as you navigate life's transitions. The Bible is your catalyst for transformation in your being and becoming.

Nexting is about who you are and who you want to be.

DIRECTION, NOT PERFECTION

> *I'm not saying that I have this all together, that I have it made. But I am well on my way, reaching out for Christ, who has so wondrously reached out for me. Friends, don't get me wrong: By no means do I count myself an expert in all of this, but I've got my eye on the goal, where God is beckoning us onward—to Jesus. I'm off and running, and I'm not turning back.—Philippians 3:12-14 (MSG)*

nexting

Knowing the direction that you are moving towards, is the key to cultivating purposefulness and boosting the resiliency necessary to enjoy the level that you are living on right now in your next. *Nexting* is the conscious anticipation of the plans of God unfolding in your life as you engage in the now!

PART III TAKEAWAYS

Experiencing Transitions: You are going from your now to your next. The plans that God has for you are unfolding before you and by grace, through faith, you are working the process. You are accepting and confirming that it is in God that you live, move, and have your being. There is a difference between existing and living, between surviving and thriving. You are proof that one can live through life transitions of change rather than just simply exist while transition happens.

The Dynamics of **Nexting**: the definition of dynamics is a pattern or process of change, growth, or activity. **Nexting** itself is dynamic and is experienced throughout the different life transitions of change.

The dynamics of v are Purpose, Vision, Passion, Timing, Stewardship, Exhortation, Wisdom, Decisiveness, and Grace.

As a Nexter, you realize that life transitions are, in essence, transformative.

Transition assistance is encouraged and accessible.

Next Is Now: Affirming the direct correlation between your now and your next and allowing your next to influence your now.

Towards: Living through the **Nexting** process as we decide who we are going to be and what we are going to do next.

CONCLUSION

Your next is worth pursuing and waiting for at the same time. *Nexting* is forward-focused and future-oriented. *Nexting* is the conscious anticipation of the plans of God unfolding in your life as you engage in the now. *Nexting* involves navigating and negotiating life transitions with the right mindset and heart-set. *Nexting* encourages you to consider the journey ahead carefully and strategically. As you reflect and prepare for your next, consider the following question, "What are the plans that God has for you that will bring you a hope and a future?" Trust that what God has planned for you and what He permits to happen in your life is full of potential and possibilities. To anticipate and develop a course of action for what lies ahead includes paying attention to where you are. The journey ahead is directly connected to the current location—your starting point. When mapping out your route to get to your desired destination, every navigational system always asks for your current location. Your now must be considered. Now impacts your next. Remember that God has plans for you; He wants to give you hope and a future. The next one up is you!

Please consider my #NEXT1UP masterclass, videos, and workbook/manual to assist you. Also, check out the *Nexting* journal entitled "NEXT NOTES" as a daily devotional to jump-start your day with reflective and inspirational thoughts. Finally, keep a lookout for my next book, entitled *Lost in Transition*. *Lost in Transition* will explore what

196 nexting

happens when you get lost in transition, the challenges of being lost in transition, and how to activate a reroute in your life.

GOD HAS A NEXT FOR YOU!

#Next1Up

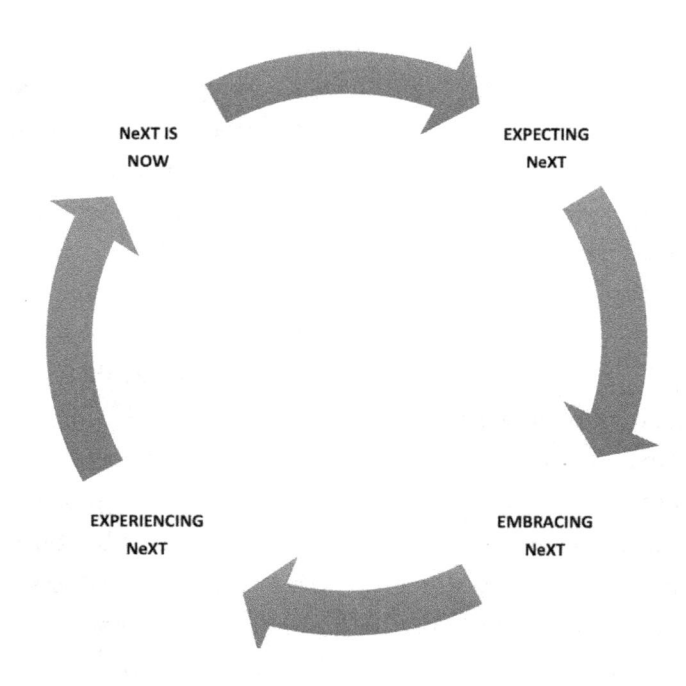

- NeXT IS NOW
- EXPECTING NeXT
- EMBRACING NeXT
- EXPERIENCING NeXT

TIM WILLIAMS

FIND MORE ABOUT TIM AND HIS SPEAKING OPPORTUNITIES AT:

(407) 414-4321

WWW.TWILEADERS.COM

INFO@TWILEADERS.COM

@twileaders

Printed in the USA
CPSIA information can be obtained
at www.ICGtesting.com
JSHW011116180524
63155JS00005B/13